HIGH LINE

HIGH LINE

The Inside Story of New York City's
Park in the Sky

Joshua David and Robert Hammond

 Farrar, Straus and Giroux
New York

Farrar, Straus and Giroux
18 West 18th Street, New York 10011

Distributed in Canada by D&M Publishers, Inc.
Printed in the United States of America
First edition, 2011

Image credits can be found on pages 335–37.

Library of Congress Cataloging-in-Publication Data
David, Joshua, 1963–
     High Line : the inside story of New York City's park In the sky /
Joshua David and Robert Hammond. — 1st ed.
        p. cm.
     Includes index.
     ISBN 978-0-374-53299-4 (paperback : alk. paper)
     1. High Line (New York, N.Y. : Park)—History. 2.
New York (N.Y.)—History. 3. Manhattan (New York, N.Y.)—History.
I. Hammond, Robert, 1969– II. Title.

F128.65.H54D38 2011
974.7'1—dc23
                                                    2011020429

Designed by Pentagram

www.fsgbooks.com

10   9   8   7   6   5   4   3

CONTENTS

VII PREFACE

VIII TIME LINE: 1847–1999

  1 HIGH LINE

  03 Mile and a Half
  09 Friends of the High Line
  16 Rails to Trails
  28 Strategy Session
  36 Demolition?
  41 At City Hall
  48 Under the Fence Tour
  53 Ideas for the High Line
  64 City Planning
  73 Four Teams, Four Visions
  81 Raise the Money
  89 Railbanked!
  93 ''I Saved the High Line''
  101 Rail Yards
  109 Why Should They Turn It Over to Us?
  118 Cutting the Ribbon

125 AFTERWORD

131 PHOTOGRAPHS

321 ACKNOWLEDGMENTS

327 INDEX

PREFACE

"A pair of nobodies who undertook [an] impossible mission": that's how a journalist writing about the High Line's unlikely success once referred to the two of us.

It's true: When we started we knew very little about preservation, architecture, community organizing, horticulture, fundraising, working with City Hall, or running a park.

Our lack of expertise was a key to the High Line's success. It forced us to ask other people to help us. It was these others, who rallied around us, guided us, and did the work we did not know how to do, who made the High Line possible.

You could talk to any of the people mentioned in this book, or any of the several thousand neighbors, volunteers, donors, designers, government representatives, and High Line staff members who've been involved in our work, and they would tell the unlikely story of the High Line differently from the way we have done. Their versions would be just as true as ours.

This book is not comprehensive. Many people who played critical roles are not mentioned by name, and many important events are not described here.

But when we walk on the High Line, we remember all the stories that lie under every part of the park. We like to think that other people can sense these hidden stories, too, and sense that the High Line is steeped in the passion of all the people who've worked together to make it what it is today.

Joshua David
Robert Hammond
New York City
August 2011

TIME LINE
1847–1999

1847

The City of New York authorizes street-level railroad tracks down Manhattan's West Side, already a bustling industrial waterfront. Soon, trains from Hudson River Rail Road and other lines begin to serve the factories and warehouses on the waterfront and along Tenth and Eleventh avenues.

1866

Conflicts between trains and street traffic are already significant. A Senate committee reports: "The traction of freight and passenger trains by ordinary locomotive on the surface of the street is an evil which has already been endured too long and must be speedily abated."

1869

Cornelius Vanderbilt consolidates his railroad holdings, including Hudson River Rail Road, to form the New York Central and Hudson River Railroad Company.

1908

Congestion of rail, ship, and street traffic strangles commercial activity on the West Side. Five hundred people protest against the dangerous conditions of **"DEATH AVENUE,"** the name used for parts of Tenth, Eleventh, and Twelfth avenues, where the trains run at grade.

1920s

As a stopgap measure to prevent further casualties until the at-grade crossings are eliminated, the railroad hires men on horses called the **WEST SIDE COWBOYS** to ride in front of trains and wave red flags to warn pedestrians.

1924

The New York City Transit Commission orders that all street-level grade crossings must be removed between Spuyten Duyvil, at Manhattan's northern tip, and West Sixtieth Street.

1925

The New York Times refers to these grade-crossing elimination plans as "the west side improvement." It later becomes the railroad and the City's official name for the project.

1927

The City and the railroad reach a preliminary agreement for the exchange of real estate and easements that will allow the removal of freight lines from New York City's streets. The railroad proposes the "erection of AN ELEVATED LINE from . . . Canal Street, north to the Thirtieth Street Yard . . ."

1929

The initial construction contract is signed, and the first spikes are removed from the "Death Avenue" tracks by Mayor Walker, "to be gold-plated and preserved as mementos of the happy end to a forty-year controversy between the city and the railroad."

1931

CONSTRUCTION BEGINS on the new structure. Teams of steelworkers assemble its massive frame by hand, driving several hundred thousand rivets through thick steel beams. Construction also begins on the 3.6-million-square-foot St. John's Park Terminal on Clarkson Street. The terminal is designed to accept 190 rail cars from the High Line directly into its second story.

1933

THE FIRST TRAIN RUNS ON THE HIGH LINE, delivering freight to the R. C. Williams & Company warehouse. At this time, the High Line is referred to simply as an elevated track. The nickname that later becomes its moniker is not commonly used before the late 1980s.

1934

THE HIGH LINE OFFICIALLY OPENS on June 28. *The New York Times* estimates its cost at $85 million. Officials herald it as "one of the greatest public improvements in the history of New York."

1934–1960

The High Line is fully operational from West Thirty-fourth Street to St. John's Park Terminal on Clarkson Street.

1960

A decline in rail traffic, due in part to the increase in freight truck traffic on the new interstate highway system, prompts the New York Central Railroad to sell St. John's Park Terminal and to halt service on the southernmost section of the High Line, south of Bank Street. Soon afterward, the City demolishes the High Line south of Bank Street.

1968
Penn Central takes over New York Central Railroad.

1976
The federal government forms Consolidated Rail Corporation, or Conrail, from the remains of six rail carriers in the Northeast and Midwest, including Penn Central. The High Line becomes Conrail's property.

1980
THE LAST TRAIN
runs down the High Line, reportedly pulling three boxcars of frozen turkeys.

1983
Conrail takes the first legal step toward divesting itself of the High Line, publishing a "notice of insufficient revenues."

The West Side Rail Line Development Foundation is formed by Chelsea resident Peter Obletz, who aims to reestablish rail service as a way of preserving the structure and its easement for future public good.

Congress passes the National Trails System Act, allowing out-of-use rail lines to be "railbanked"—used as pedestrian or bike trails while held for future transportation needs. Because a railbanked corridor is not considered abandoned, it can be sold, leased, or donated to a trail manager without the property rights reverting to underlying landowners.

The High Line captures the imagination of local architect Steven Holl, whose innovative scheme, "Bridge of Houses," proposes to repurpose the structure for housing, commerce, and open space.

1984
Obletz's group applies to purchase the High Line for future rail use. The bid is approved by the Interstate Commerce Commission (ICC). Obletz negotiates to BUY THE LINE FROM CONRAIL FOR TEN DOLLARS and begins fending off challenges from the State and a group of underlying landowners, which eventually adopts the name Chelsea Property Owners.

Amtrak begins negotiating to run trains on the line's easement north of West Thirty-fourth Street. When the deal and resulting construction is ultimately completed in the early 1990s, it will allow Amtrak to use the former freight line for passenger service and consolidate its operations at Penn Station.

1986
The City files papers with the ICC opposing the acquisition of the High Line by Peter Obletz. Soon afterward, the ICC reverses its earlier decision: it now believes that Obletz and his foundation do not have the resources to run a working railroad. The sale agreement is nullified.

1989

Chelsea Property Owners files an application to the ICC requesting an adverse abandonment order for the High Line, which would require Conrail to involuntarily abandon and demolish it.

1991

Rockrose Development Corporation DEMOLISHES THE SOUTHERNMOST FIVE BLOCKS OF THE HIGH LINE in order to convert a former industrial warehouse into an apartment complex. This brings the structure's terminus to Gansevoort Street, in the Meatpacking District.

1999

CSX Transportation assumes control of Conrail. Shortly after assuming ownership of the High Line, CSX commissions a Regional Plan Association (RPA) study on feasible reuse alternatives. RPA rejects the use of the High Line for subway, bus, or truck transit, as well as waste transfer facility and a commuter rail storage facility. The study recommends focusing on light-rail and greenway use instead.

JULY 1999

In a *New York Times* article, a CSX representative declares that the company is amenable to considering reuse proposals for the line.

AUGUST 1999

After reading the *New York Times* article, West Village resident Robert Hammond and Chelsea resident Joshua David attend a High Line–focused community hearing at Penn South in Chelsea. Robert and Joshua, who do not know each other, are each interested in helping to save the High Line from demolition. Within months, they cofound FRIENDS OF THE HIGH LINE.

HIGH LINE

Mile and a Half

ROBERT

I graduated from college in 1993, and the next year I moved to the West Village, an apartment at Tenth Street and Washington. I was attracted to the West Village because it was a jumble of different parts of New York. It still had an industrial character. It had old and new residential buildings. It had the Hudson River, which had not yet been transformed into a park. The piers were still rotting.

I used to go out a lot in the neighborhood, and there was a bar a few blocks from where I lived called Automatic Slim's. On the wall outside the bar, they had posted an old black-and-white photo of a train running through a factory building. If you looked across the street, you could see the building that was in the photo, where the train used to run through at the third-floor level.

You could still see the tracks, cut off on both sides. When I was walking in the neighborhood, I'd stop and look at the picture and then look up at the building. I liked the idea that a train used to run through my neighborhood.

JOSH

When my boyfriend, Stephen, and I moved to Chelsea in 1986, nobody paid much notice to anything west of Tenth Avenue, except some gay bars.

The first night we spent in the apartment we live in now was in 1993. Our front room is a little bit below the sidewalk level, so when you look out, you see people walking on Twenty-first Street from the waist down.

It was summer, and I was on my hands and knees painting the floor. I looked out and saw this parade of male legs in very short shorts going past the window. A club called Zone DK was over in that direction, just before the West Side Highway. It was a dark, gay place where people would go into the shadows and things would happen. The Spike and the Eagle were over there, too. We liked the Spike. We never went to the Eagle very much.

The High Line was about a block from our door. It came out from behind the Church of the Guardian Angel, bridged across Twenty-first Street, and then disappeared behind some tenement buildings. I never paid it much attention.

ROBERT

I also spent some time in the Meatpacking District—I'd gone to the restaurant Florent—and I had seen parts of the High Line in that neighborhood. And I had gone to a few galleries in Chelsea and seen it cross over the streets there. But I'd never realized all the bits and pieces were connected.

JOSH

I had my grandmother's old Buick parked near the rail yards. The High Line was over there, too; there used to be a lot of hookers underneath it. I never made the connection—that that dark metal bridge with all the hookers at Twenty-eighth Street was the same thing that crossed Twenty-first Street—because most of the High Line was hidden behind buildings.

ROBERT

I had been a history major in college, and my first job after that was at Ernst & Young, doing consulting. I got bored pretty quickly and left. Over the next few years, I worked for a variety of start-ups. I helped start an in-flight catalog, a competitor to *SkyMall*. We were selling nose hair trimmers out of airplanes. I helped launch an HIV/AIDS website called thebody.com.

I was also a part-time, self-taught painter. I had had a few small shows. So I had an artistic side, but my background was in business.

JOSH

If you look at old maps of Manhattan, you'll see a jagged dotted line that traces the natural shoreline. East of Tenth Avenue is residential, the nice town house blocks of Chelsea. West of Tenth, everything is built on landfill, and the neighborhood and industry developed around the railroad.

It started changing in the mid-1980s. The Kitchen, a center for video, music, dance, and other arts, came in on West Nineteenth Street around 1985. The Dia Center for the Arts came in on West Twenty-second Street around 1987. Then the galleries started coming in the early to mid-1990s: Paula Cooper, Matthew Marks, and Barbara Gladstone. By 1999 the galleries had grown to a significant number, and the Comme des Garçons store opened on West Twenty-second Street. That was a trigger for fashion magazines, style magazines, and design magazines to turn their attention to the neighborhood, and I got assigned an article about changes happening in West Chelsea.

The world of these magazines was one I knew well. I'd been a freelance writer for fifteen years, and I'd occasionally take an editing gig at *Vanity Fair*, *Gourmet*, *Redbook*, or *Brides*, and I did some cater-waitering on the side. I'd done a lot of travel writing, but I was trying to break out of the travel ghetto, making a conscious effort to take only stories that were of interest to me, about architecture if possible. When I was in college, at Penn, I wanted to be an architect, and I took the first required course for that degree, Design of Environment. The professor brought us outside on the lawn to draw buildings and trees. He said I would never be an architect because the leaves on my trees were so badly drawn.

ROBERT

The summer of 1999, I read a piece in *The New York Times* that said that Mayor Giuliani's administration was trying to tear down the High Line. The *Times* ran a little map of it, and you could see that the High Line was continuous, a mile and a half of rail tracks running right through Manhattan. That's what really got me interested in it, the idea that this industrial relic had lasted so long and was about to be torn down.

Around this time, I was hired by a retailer called Watch World to start their Internet division. It was the first time in my life that I had my own office with a door to close, and so it was the first time I could do things besides work at work. So I decided to get involved with the High Line somehow.

My first thought was that I could help someone else who was already working on it. This is New York, and in New York everything that could ever be threatened has a group associated with it, right? So I started making some calls to people involved in civic projects, asking them if they knew who the group was.

I called Gifford Miller, a good friend of mine from college who had been elected to the City Council on the Upper East Side. He basically told me that trying to save an old rail line was a stupid idea. But I kept calling around. I called the local community board and talked to Ed Kirkland, who was the head of the Preservation and Planning Committee. He wasn't that excited about the idea of saving the High Line, and he said he didn't know anyone else who was. But he called back later in the summer and told me there was a community board hearing on the High Line scheduled for a night in August.

JOSH

I walked up and down all the blocks in West Chelsea researching my article. The place where Printed Matter is now, on Twenty-second and Tenth, used be an intercom store; they sold front-door intercom systems for apartment buildings. And there was a Formica maker, and glass cutters, and a whole bunch of industrial suppliers that are now almost entirely gone.

That is when I began paying attention to the High Line, really looking up at it for the first time, because it was everywhere, running over every block. It was about thirty feet tall, and you couldn't see what was on top of it, but the rusting Art Deco railings gave it a sense of lost beauty, and the spaces underneath were very dramatic; they had a dark, gritty, industrial quality, and a lofty, church-like quality as well. In the heat of summer, it was shadowy and cool underneath. I didn't know what the thing was called then. My friend John told me it was a sex spot— coming out of the Spike or the Eagle, he'd ducked underneath it with a trick more than once. There was sex to be had up on top, too, and there were parties up there, raves, along with some homeless encampments.

As I asked more people about it, I ended up calling a guy I'd seen at block association meetings, Ed Kirkland, who'd lived in the neighborhood for many years and knew everything there was to know about Chelsea.

Ed told me that it ran from Gansevoort Street to Thirty-fourth Street without a break in it. They had torn down pieces of it south of Gansevoort Street; a piece from Clarkson to Bethune Street had been demolished in the 1960s, and the piece between Bethune and Gansevoort Street had been taken down in 1991, but what was left north of Gansevoort Street was intact and still technically a working railroad, even though no trains ran on it. Anybody who looked at it would say it was abandoned; but it had not been "abandoned," which is a formal railroad term; it was still a functioning rail easement that could connect into the old New York Central tracks up to Albany.

That was the trigger for me—that it was so big and that it was unbroken for twenty-two blocks. I had assumed that somebody at some point would have torn down a part of it to build something else, that it was a collection of relics, but it was a single relic, all in one piece.

I felt what I think is the spark of most people's interest in the High Line: Wouldn't it be cool to walk around up there, twenty-two city blocks, on this old, elevated thing, on this relic of another time, in this hidden place, up in the air?

Right around then the *Times* ran its article saying that the High Line had been acquired by CSX, the railroad company, that the City wanted to tear it down, and that CSX was open to rail-trail proposals. I called people who were quoted in the article and asked them: Were there any organizations working on this? There were none—no historical groups, no parks groups, nobody.

One of the people quoted in the article was a CSX represent-ative, Debra Frank. Debra told me that CSX had commissioned a study about the High Line and that they were going to present it at a community board meeting.

I was off from work that week, out on Fire Island, and I actually came back from the beach to go to that meeting. I had never been to a community board meeting before. I had never had any desire to go to a community board meeting before.

The meeting was held in a room at Penn South in mid-August—one of those lazy, hot, late summer evenings in New York where anybody who has the ability not to be in the city is not in the city.

The Penn South complex was built in the 1950s as housing for members of the Garment Workers' Union. There are now a lot of senior citizens in these buildings. It is a world unto itself: no stores, not much signage, nothing on street level to invite people in. The community room, roughly at Twenty-seventh Street and Eighth Avenue, was a hard room to find.

I sat next to Robert because I thought he was cute. Community board meetings are not necessarily filled with cute guys, so I said to myself, Well, there's one, why don't I sit next to him?

There were maybe twenty people at the meeting. It began with a presentation by someone from the Regional Plan Association, which had been commissioned by CSX to do a study of the possible uses for the High Line. They presented some different options, from demolition to using it for freight to making a park up on top of it. And they mentioned the federal Rails-to-Trails program.

After the RPA presented, a bunch of people got up and spoke about why it was a bad idea to reuse the High Line. A guy named Doug Sarini spoke, representing a group of property owners in Chelsea who had been working for fifteen years to tear it down. He said it was a blight on the neighborhood. It was going to fall down any day. It was holding up the economic development of the area. It was dangerous. It was dark underneath. A whole litany of arguments, and really vehement. I was surprised at how strongly these people felt. I had been thinking about speaking at the meeting, but not after all that.

I stayed behind afterward, trying to find anyone else who was interested in saving the High Line. There was no one except the guy who had been sitting next to me. He told me his name was Josh, that he lived in the neighborhood, that he was a travel writer.

I said something like "Well, you know, I'm very busy, but if you start something, I could help." And he said, "Well, I'm also very busy. Maybe you should start something." We exchanged business cards and agreed to talk later.

JOSH

People exchange cards all the time and nothing happens. If I think of all the times I exchanged business cards with somebody in New York City and something happened afterward, it's a very small number.

ROBERT

So that was the genesis of Friends of the High Line, that first community board meeting where no one else was interested in trying to save it. I think we had both looked around, realized no one else was doing anything, and that if something was going to be done, we would need to start it ourselves.

JOSH

Robert had a temporary-feeling office near Herald Square, and that's where we met a few weeks later. I don't think either of us knew exactly what we were trying to accomplish, beyond trying to see if there was something better to do with the High Line than just tear it down. We already had enough of a sense from that one meeting that this was going to be a huge endeavor, and each of us tried to get the other to do it. Neither of us wanted to be the one who owned it.

ROBERT

I didn't understand the complexity of what we were getting into—that we would soon be swimming in an alphabet soup of CITUs, STBs, ULURPs, and RFPs; that we would need to become versed in urban planning, architecture, and City politics, raise millions of dollars, and give years of our lives to the High Line. I had no idea that this would become a vocation, and I didn't want it to. I had no background for it. I was enjoying building my career.

JOSH

The RPA study had said that making the High Line a park was probably the most appealing, least complicated way of reusing it. That idea appealed to us, in part, I think because we just wanted to figure out a way for people to go up there. We figured that the first step in starting an organization for this would be naming it. High Line Park Association was one name we came up with.

ROBERT

My mother asked me, "What are the chances?" I said, "One in a hundred." She asked, "Well, should you be spending your time on it, then?"

Friends of the High Line

JOSH

I left town after Labor Day. I had an assignment to do a cross-country trip for a magazine, *Travel Holiday*, tracing the Lincoln Highway, America's first cross-country highway, built in the early 1900s: each state made its own little two-lane road and then they were cobbled together. In some places, you could find the old two-lane road, but most of it had been swallowed up by suburbia or bigger highways.

Along the way, I'd meet people who were interested in preserving what was left of the highway. They'd started these little Lincoln Highway societies.

I stayed overnight with a couple in Iowa—farmers, a husband and wife—who were heads of their local group. They drove me around and showed me their part of the Lincoln Highway and its WPA-era concrete bridges and told me about what they had gone through to get it listed on the National Register of Historic Places.

These were farmers in Iowa. They had no preservation training. But they had gotten their part of the road designated and were writing pamphlets about it and putting up signs and raising money to do little projects.

I thought, if they can do this, I can do it. It doesn't require any particular knowledge.

ROBERT

Mario Palumbo, my best friend from college, was working with Phil Aarons, a developer who had worked in City government during the Koch administration. Phil and his wife, Shelley, were involved in a lot of art causes and quirky nonprofits.

I went to dinner with Mario and Phil and Shelley. Phil had looked at the High Line when he was working for Mayor Koch, at EDC, the New York City Economic Development Corporation. He was discouraging at first, but the next day he e-mailed me some research he'd done on the High Line after our dinner. I kept going back to him. A lot of what he does is build complicated real estate projects—Ritz-Carltons and Four Seasons all over the country.

In September, I went on a vacation to Europe with Mario for my thirtieth birthday. We met up with Phil and Shelley in Germany, and Mario kept pushing me to move the High Line project forward.

JOSH

In the beginning I was suspicious of Phil's involvement. What little I knew about community activism in New York was that the real estate guys were the bad guys: you were always fighting the real estate guys, you were never working with them.

ROBERT

Josh and I were very different. I was in business, and liked
business. I thought of him as a community guy, very grassroots,
very anti-development—a classic New York liberal, in the best
sense of the term.

JOSH

Robert had a studio in the Starrett-Lehigh Building, where he
painted. It was a weird place: not really a room, almost a hallway,
long and skinny, with south-facing windows that looked over
West Chelsea and the river. There was one chair. One person
got to sit and everyone else stood or leaned against the wall.
Looking out the window, you could see bits of the High Line,
popping from behind buildings, crossing the streets, and
disappearing again. I met Mario and Phil there, and we talked. I
was struck by how good-looking Mario was. It was obvious that
Phil had a nuanced understanding of how things like the High
Line could happen. When we talked about making it a park, he
said it might not actually be a park, that there were all kinds of
public spaces in New York, created through zoning, that were
privately owned. They might look like parks and feel like parks,
but they were not really parks.

    After the meeting we went down to the street, where there
was a black car waiting. Phil was the first person I knew who
often had a black car waiting.

ROBERT

Phil, Josh, and I got a meeting with Debra Frank from CSX. We
were so excited that the railroad was meeting with us. The
meeting was on a high floor in the World Trade Center. I
remember looking out the window to the north, such a classic
New York vista. You couldn't see the High Line from there, but I
remember having a thought about the High Line: rarely do
people get to change the way New York looks from the sky.

JOSH

David Richards, CSX's lawyer, was there, and Debra. We told
them we were interested in the trail-use idea for the High Line,
and they gave us some background.

    There was a conditional abandonment order from the STB,
the Surface Transportation Board. The ruling went back to 1992.
It had originally been issued by the ICC, or Interstate Commerce
Commission, which handled federal oversight of railroads
before the STB came along. The conditional abandonment order
meant that the High Line could be torn down if certain conditions
were met: The property owners had to guarantee there was
enough money in place to tear it down and cover all liability.
The railroad would be required to contribute $7 million, but the
property owners still hadn't assembled the financial guarantee

to cover all demolition costs beyond that plus the liability. Nobody knew how much it would cost to tear it down. Some people said it might cost $20 million or $30 million.

Debra also explained the railroad's position on the High Line: they were basically neutral. "CSX wants to get out of the High Line business" was how Debra phrased it. They had to pay taxes on it, they had to maintain it, there was liability associated with it, and they didn't see a future use for it. But the way in which it was gotten rid of—that they were neutral on. If tearing it down ended up being the best scenario, they were open to that. If the best scenario was turning it into a park, they were open to that. They would continue to work with both sides.

ROBERT

We went up to Windows on the World and Phil ordered glasses of champagne for us. We were so naïvely optimistic: we thought we could just get the ball rolling and it would happen. We were also trying to figure out what to call the group.

JOSH

Phil said it couldn't be High Line Park Association, because the High Line might not end up being a park. We offered some of the other names we'd thought of—"preservation" this or "coalition" that: community group names—but Phil said you had to think of how City officials would look at you, how the real estate people would look at you. He said you wanted the name to be as neutral as possible, and he suggested Friends of the High Line. Friends groups are common: there are "friends" of all sorts of things. This name was friendly; it didn't have the word *park* or *preservation* in it—there were no lightning rods. I don't know if I loved it at the time, but I understood Phil's logic.

ROBERT

I didn't like "Friends of the High Line" as we were picking it. I wanted something different. But we sort of settled on it, over that drink.

JOSH

So we toasted and left. That was my first and last visit to Windows on the World.

ROBERT

Debra Frank brought us up to the High Line the first time. We went up through Chelsea Market, which had opened a year or so earlier and was still a pretty sleepy place. We met down at the western end of the concourse—Debra Frank, Ed Kirkland, Josh, me, and a couple of others.

JOSH

We went outside the building and around to a truck bay on Sixteenth Street. There was a loading dock and a freight elevator covered inside with pinup girl pictures—actresses you had never seen in anything, just hot babes. You would ride that elevator to the third floor and the old train platform, where the trains used to load and unload for the Nabisco factory that once was in Chelsea Market.

Irwin Cohen, creator of Chelsea Market, was a great collector of urban artifacts. He originally decorated Chelsea Market with lots of old lampposts and salvaged metal things. The storehouse for all this junk was up on this platform. There was also an artist who worked there—a metalworker—and Irwin allowed him to use the platform as a studio. So there were all these rusty metal sculptures. The place was covered in graffiti.

ROBERT

You walked out, and you were on train tracks that were covered in wildflowers. I don't know what I had expected. Maybe just gravel, stone ballast, and tracks—more of a ruin. Maybe I thought it would be full of homeless people. I just didn't expect wildflowers. This was not a few blades of grass growing up through gravel. The wildflowers and plants had taken over. We had to wade through waist-high Queen Anne's lace. It was another world, right in the middle of Manhattan.

JOSH

We went north, to the square over Tenth Avenue. On one side, you could see the Hudson River, out to the Statue of Liberty. On the other side, you could lean on the railing and watch the cars on Tenth Avenue flowing underneath you. Then we rounded a curve and discovered, stretching out in front of us, this incredible straightaway that went all the way from Seventeenth Street up to Thirtieth Street, thirteen blocks long, with a view of the Empire State Building. It was a shock to see how beautiful it was. There was this tremendous sense of space. I'd passed it a million times and I hadn't known it was there, hidden away in plain sight.

You think of hidden things as small. That is how they stay hidden. But this hidden thing was huge. A huge space in New York City that had somehow escaped everybody's notice.

Those early visits locked the place in Robert's and my minds. Something amazing could happen up here.

There was a powerful sense of the passing of time. You could see what the High Line was built for, and feel that its moment had slipped away. All the buildings alongside it were brick warehouses and factories with smokestacks and casement windows, like buildings from a Hopper painting.

ROBERT

Seeing it for the first time made us realize how important it was to show it to other people. It was the only way for others to really understand it. Debra Frank allowed us to invite people up from time to time—people from the community, or in government, or from civic groups. A few would say, "This just looks like a field of weeds; they should tear this down." But most people were moved by it. You brought them up, you showed it to them, and they would do anything for the High Line after that.

Saving the High Line and making a park out of it might have seemed like a crazy idea, but this was during the dot-com boom. Kids in their twenties were taking small start-up companies public for huge sums.

There was another project I was thinking of starting at the same time. It would be a new kind of business school, for one year instead of two. I had files for both projects in my desk, my two crazy ideas.

JOSH

When you look at our first year, so much of what we did was just learn the landscape. The project had a national level and a City government level. Then there was the railroad to deal with, and the community. Our most daunting opponents were the property owners who'd backed the demolition effort for years. There were more than twenty of them, and most of them had bought their land at prices that reflected that the land had an old railroad structure over it—cheap land in a manufacturing district. Yet there was the understanding that, with manufacturing on the decline, there would be a rezoning, and residential development would be permitted. They hoped to increase their value exponentially by forcing the railroad to tear down the High Line so they could build in that space.

We weren't in a good position with the Giuliani administration. Joe Rose, the chair of the Planning Commission, had taken a strong position to the High Line in that first *Times* article. He said, "The High Line is the Vietnam of old railroad structures . . . It must come down." Phil knew Joe, and he called him early on to see if there was a chance the City would change its position, but Joe told him the decision had been made. It was coming down.

ROBERT

In college I had rowed lightweight crew for three years. I was the shortest, lightest guy on the team, not tall enough to be very good. But I was determined to do it. In my first year, I was in an undefeated boat, and I kept doing it, even though I never enjoyed it.

I look back on crew as an example of a trap I got into, of pursuing a challenge for the challenge's sake. I worried that the High Line was the same kind of thing.

JOSH

My good friend Joyce Pierpoline used to live in Paris. She said, "You know, there is something like the High Line there."

I was already set to go to Paris for Thanksgiving; my uncle and grandmother live there. So I went to Paris and visited the Promenade Plantée, near the Bastille opera house. It had been completed just a few years earlier. It was on a different kind of elevated rail structure—older, made of masonry arches instead of steel. Walking up the stairs and stepping into that park was amazing. People had done this, they had built stairs, and now people were going up them and using this elevated park. It had become part of the neighborhood. So it was not a totally insane idea. It had happened in Paris, and it could happen in New York City.

ROBERT

Mario took the lead in getting us legally incorporated as a nonprofit—he asked lawyers from his firm to do it pro bono. He called me up and said, "I need a list of officers. Who are the officers?" It seems obvious now that Josh and I were always running it, but at that time I thought maybe Mario should run it. He was spending as much time on it as I was and had more relevant experience. But he was busier than Josh and I were. So the compromise was that all three of us would be officers.

We needed a board, too. We had been kicking the High Line idea around with a lot of people. Many of them were people I'd met through Mario and Phil. So our first board members were Phil; Mario; Josh; me; an architect named Gary Handel, who had designed buildings for Phil; and Olivia Douglas, another colleague of Mario's and Phil's.

Around this time, we brought Gifford Miller up for a tour, and he fell in love with it. I think he recognized its potential, and immediately wanted to help. The High Line would have never happened without Gifford.

JOSH

Phil told us we needed to announce to the community board what we were doing. The High Line runs through two community board districts, Board 2 and Board 4. Robert lives in Board 2, so he went to the Board 2 meeting, and I live in Board 4, so I went to the Board 4 meeting.

The full board meeting was bigger than the committee meeting where Robert and I had met—about forty-five people sitting around a U-shaped table, and an audience of one hundred. I had never talked in front of that many people before. I went to the mike and said, "My name is Joshua David, and Robert Hammond and I have started a group called Friends of the High Line. We want save the High Line so that the public can go up and enjoy the beautiful space that is up there."

Some people reacted positively, but there were challenging questions right off the bat. "How much is that going to cost? Aren't pieces of it already falling off? Won't people commit suicide jumping from it?" I began to understand that this was not going to be a universally beloved project.

Christine Quinn, our local City Council member, was there. I knew her a bit—a few years earlier I had volunteered on a campaign for Tom Duane that she had managed. I went up to her and said, "We want to save the High Line." She said, "Oh, I love the High Line."

ROBERT

We sent Christine Quinn a packet of information about the High Line that Josh had put together. It wasn't much, just some basics about the legal status of the High Line and nice-sounding text about how good it would be to save it—a new park for a neighborhood without many parks, a piece of our industrial heritage. Later she told us, "I have a file in my district office labeled 'Good Ideas That Will Never Happen.' That is where we put your stuff. But the file kept getting bigger and bigger, and we had to give you a file of your own."

JOSH

We had both been in New York long enough to know that what the press wants is famous people, or at least well-known people. So we started thinking about people we could get. The first ones we thought of were the gallery people. They were in the neighborhood.

I was not an art world follower, but as a cater-waiter I had waited on Paula Cooper's table once at a Guggenheim benefit, and I knew she was one of the first gallery owners to have come to West Chelsea. I wrote a letter—"Can we use your name as a supporter?"—put together a package of information, and dropped it all off at the gallery. Her assistant, Ona, called to tell me Paula had said yes. I couldn't believe she'd signed on.

I also dropped a packet off at Matthew Marks's gallery. He said yes, too.

I went to a presentation at the Municipal Art Society where Richard Meier was a panelist. I hadn't gone to see Richard Meier—I'd gone to see someone else—but I heard him speak, and I thought, oh, he seems like a big, important architect. So after the panel, I sent him a little note about what we were doing, and he signed on.

This is what we did at first: collect names of people who we could say supported our idea. We didn't have an office, we didn't have a phone number, we didn't have a mailbox—we didn't have anything, just names.

For the first year, our goal was to get another organization to take the High Line on—the Municipal Art Society, or the Van Alen Institute, or the Architectural League.

It was in the winter of 1999 when we met with the Municipal Art Society. Phil, Josh, and I went, with the architect Gary Handel, who'd put together presentation boards. It was a big meeting, with Frank Sanchis, one of the heads of MAS, in a wood-paneled library on the second floor of the Villard Houses, on Madison Avenue. Lynden Miller, Gifford's mother, went with us. She was a famous garden designer and she gave us a lot of credibility.

After the meeting, Frank took our proposal to the MAS board. He told us that MAS wouldn't be able to take on the project itself, but that it would try to help us, and would come out to community board meetings in support.

We started to realize that no one else was going to do this for us.

Rails to Trails

JOSH

Jeff Ciabotti at the Rails-to-Trails Conservancy, in Washington, explained the term *railbanking* to me, and it quickly became central to our plan. Railbanking is one of the ways that you can create a trail on an old rail line. Maybe you've been on a trail in a state forest that used to be a railroad. It's easy to create a public trail in a place like that, because the government owns the land underneath the rails. When you take away the tracks and the easement, the government still owns the corridor and can turn it into a trail.

But a lot of corridors go over private land. When those easements were created, the contracts usually stipulated that the easement was for rail use only. So if you took away the rail use, you couldn't use the easement for something else. The corridor would vanish—and the underlying owner could reclaim the property.

The federal government realized that when rail corridors were being lost in this way, we were also losing national assets. So in 1983 they passed an amendment to the National Trails System Act that included a "railbanking" statute. This stipulated that rail easements could be used for "interim trail use." Essentially, the government set up a system to "bank" out-of-use rail corridors as trails, because the country might need them again for rail use in the future.

To make this happen for the High Line, we had to get the holy grail: a Certificate of Interim Trail Use, or CITU. If the

Surface Transportation Board issued one of these, it meant we could work with the railroad to railbank the High Line.

But the STB had gone pretty far in the opposite direction with the 1992 "conditional abandonment order." Our job was to pull the High Line back from the brink, turn the process around, and get this same federal board to say, "Okay, we won't tear it down. Let's make it a trail instead."

From that point on, whenever we made our list of goals for the year, at the top of the list would be: This year, we are going to get a CITU. We had no idea how difficult it would be.

ROBERT

For Watch World's Internet launch, we wanted to rebrand the company and get a new logo. Years before, I had come across a book of designs by the firm Pentagram. I loved the graphics and logo projects they had done, and decided to interview them for the Watch World job.

When I called them, the receptionist recommended that I talk to one of the partners, Paula Scher. Watch World's CEO and I met with Paula at Pentagram's studio, where she gave us a pitch. When I was leaving, I took Paula aside and told her I was starting this little nonprofit that was trying to turn an old elevated rail line into a park. I asked if she would help.

I don't know if it was because she wanted my business at Watch World or if she just thought it was a fun idea, but a few weeks later she sent us some Friends of the High Line logos to choose from. One was a green circle with a railroad crossing. There was another one that looked like a big H, with an extra cross-piece in it. I liked this one, because my last name is Hammond. I had a belt buckle with a big H on it at the time. It was Paula's favorite, too, and everyone we showed it to liked it best.

Paula designed business cards and stationery with that logo for us. Around that time, someone nicknamed us "two guys and a logo." We didn't have a lot else going for us. But one of the keys to the High Line's success was in always showing progress, even if it was a really small step. On those original business cards, Josh and I listed our home addresses and home phone numbers. The logo made the High Line look like it a real project. It also showed that we were committed to design—we weren't going to just put some planters up there, put up some stairs, and call it a day.

Design united a lot of our early supporters, and not just graphic design, not just architecture, but design in a bigger sense—thoughtful design, thoughtful planning. That's a word Phil used all the time when we were first starting out: *thoughtful*.

JOSH

New Year's Eve was a big deal that year. There was the Y2K scare. Everyone thought the computers were going to crash in the turnover from 1999 to 2000, that systems would halt and the world would end. The city was in total police-state mode, so Stephen and I went to St. John for New Year's week, with our friends Deborah and Joyce. People were introspective at this time, with the changing of the millennium, wondering how things might be different in the 2000s. One day on the beach in St. John, I told Deborah, whom I'd known since high school, that I felt my life was changing. For fifteen years, I'd been writing for glossy magazines about fancy hotels and foreign cities and expensive restaurants and pretty furniture. I was ready for something more substantial. Maybe it was the High Line; maybe it was something else.

ROBERT

We wanted to photograph it. We had been up there and seen this incredible wildscape—seen the city in a whole new way—but people couldn't see it from the street, and our own snapshots didn't capture it.

I mentioned our need for photos to Ray Gastil, at the Van Alen Institute. Van Alen does design competitions, and I thought they could do a design competition for the High Line. Ray was interested, but he said Van Alen had been criticized for always doing competitions for things that never got built.

Ray said, "Why don't you call Joel Sternfeld for your photos?" He said Joel had been a Rome Prize winner and had taken pictures of the aqueducts outside of Rome, and some other industrial-landscape photographs.

I looked Joel up on the Web. The only picture of his I could find was of a car that had fallen into a ravine. I found his number in the phone book and called him. I told him I'd like him to take pictures of the High Line—was he interested? CSX gave us permission to go up again. As soon as Joel saw it, he took me aside and said, "I want to do this. Don't let anyone else up here for a year. I will give you beautiful photos."

I told him what we wanted was the money shot. He has always laughed about that. I didn't know where the term *money shot* came from. I just knew it was the most important shot. I didn't know it was from porn. He said, "I'll give you your money shot."

We got permission for Joel to go up there by himself, anytime he wanted, to photograph the High Line for a year—from April 2000 to July 2001. He shot it in all four seasons. Every once in a while he'd send us a sample image. They looked good to me. We had no idea at the time that these photos would come to define the project and would propel it forward the way they did.

Later, I found out that Joel was a famous photographer.

JOSH

The local newspaper, *The Villager*, ran an article about our early efforts. It included discouraging quotes from Doug Sarini, the representative of the Chelsea Property Owners. The issue was now big enough in the neighborhood that Community Board 4 had decided to hold a public hearing on it.

Robert sent out a lot of e-mails to get supporters to come to the hearing. He had started an e-mail database through a free list program called eGroups. Whenever he or I met someone, we'd add their e-mail address to the list. But a lot of people still weren't connected; Google had launched only the year before. So I also made flyers and taped them to every lamppost in the neighborhood. I thought that the more flyers I posted, the more people would come out to support us.

The hearing was held in a big community meeting room in the Robert Fulton Houses, on Ninth Avenue. On the High Line's side, the panel included Robert, Mario, me, and Laura Hansen, from MAS—Laura was working on a project at MAS called Place Matters, about threatened buildings and businesses that gave character to their communities. Doug Sarini was on the other side.

ROBERT

Mario and I had planned what to wear. Mario was going to wear a suit, and I was going to wear jeans. That way it would look like we had someone with business smarts and someone who was the community guy.

JOSH

Pam Frederick, who was head of the community board, had taken a lot of photographs on the High Line, and she projected those—slides in a carousel, which was still the norm. Pam liked the High Line, but the slides made it look like a bunch of weeds in an abandoned lot.

Then Robert and Mario and I talked about our plans to save the High Line and make it a park—plans that weren't all that evolved yet.

Then Doug Sarini got up and did the "How Terrible the High Line Is" speech that we had heard him give at the original meeting. Only he gave it bigger and with more power this time.

Then the meeting was opened up for public comment.

We sat at the table getting paler and paler as person after person stood up and cited all the reasons they thought the High Line should be torn down. We got slammed.

ROBERT

To me it sounded romantic: a train running through your neighborhood. But to people who had lived there when the High Line was running, it wasn't romantic. They didn't just live on the wrong side of the tracks; they lived *under* the tracks. It was loud. It was dirty.

JOSH

There was a sweet-looking white-haired woman whom I'd often seen around the neighborhood, immaculately dressed, with her hair done. I thought of her as the church lady because she was a parishioner at Church of the Guardian Angel. She stood up and read from a handwritten page, saying she still lived in the same apartment in Chelsea that she'd been born in, just down the street from the High Line. She remembered the trains running and how awful they were. The High Line was cutting off Chelsea from the river and should be torn down.

The church lady was against us.

ROBERT

Some people saw the High Line as that dark thing they had to run under to avoid getting shit on by the pigeons that roosted between the girders. This was one of the biggest complaints we heard about the High Line: pigeon shit.

People also felt that it looked intimidating and dangerous. My favorite objection was when someone said that the High Line project was potentially homophobic because if you allowed people to go up there they might throw things down at gay people and transvestites.

JOSH

There was an early pioneer group in Chelsea—people who'd bought town houses in the 1970s for $30,000 and $50,000. The tree-lined streets of Chelsea exist today because those people planted trees. They loved the town house district east of Tenth Avenue, but they didn't love the industrial district west of Tenth Avenue, which they associated with the High Line. Part of the issue was the nightclubs—people puked in town house doorways coming home from clubs, and there were shootings. Also, industrial buildings aren't usually embraced by community groups. Elevated structures are vilified because they divide communities. It was said the High Line was another one of these massive structures that chopped a community in half, like the Cross-Bronx Expressway.

ROBERT

A lot of them had seen Peter Obletz try to save the High Line before us. He had been chair of the community board. He had a rail background and a plan to reinstate trains on the High Line. He even owned the High Line for a while—he bought it from the railroad for ten dollars, but the transaction was overturned in court. Peter had an organization called West Side Railroad Coalition, but when he passed away in the mid 1990s, that organization stopped operating. So the community had gone through the whole "Save the High Line" thing before. It was fresh and exciting and new to Josh and me, but it was not fresh and exciting to them.

JOSH

Ed Kirkland was at that hearing; he was at every community meeting. Ed tended to share his comments with Robert and me on the sidelines, rather than broadcasting them to the group. He liked the preservation aspect of our work, but he was worried that it would lead to high-rises in the neighborhood. Tall buildings were the enemy. In 1989 a building called the Grand Chelsea was built on Eighth Avenue. It's really the only "high rise" below Twenty-third Street—twenty stories maybe. The neighborhood erupted. The sense was that developers were coming in to build high-rises everywhere. So the neighborhood set about doing a community-led rezoning called the Chelsea Plan to stop the high-rises, which was passed right as we started the High Line project. The community succeeded in down-zoning most of Chelsea between Seventh and Tenth avenues and setting height restrictions of seven stories. But at roughly the same time, they had to accept a rezoning of the old Flower District, which allowed a corridor of thirty-five-story apartment towers to be built on Sixth Avenue north of Twenty-third Street.

Ed's worry was that if you saved the High Line, what didn't get built on the High Line sites would have to be added to what was built somewhere else, leading to taller buildings. It was a sophisticated understanding of the way a planning process might play out—a community organizer's perspective, based on experience, that in New York City, development has to go somewhere.

ROBERT

That first hearing was tough for Josh and me. But the key to starting anything is being comfortable with lots of rejection. My background was in sales. I used to set rejection targets, and I had to get rejected so many times a day or I wasn't asking enough.

JOSH

Robert was a great phoner of people, a bringer of people into things. From when he worked at start-ups, he liked doing cold calls, making lists of people and just calling them up. I couldn't do that. It would take me forever to get up the courage to call somebody to ask them for help. What I brought were my skills as a writer. I produced all our written materials. I also had a journalist's sensibility for ferreting out information, which was useful for the research we needed to do.

ROBERT

Josh would sometimes be out of town for a long time for an article, so there were periods when I would be doing a lot of the work. Then he would get back and do a lot of work, and I would focus on my business for a while.

JOSH

"Send me some stuff" is what people would say if you asked them to get involved. So we had to make "stuff." In the beginning it was just a letter. Then it got to be a long letter with an attachment. Then we knew we had to print something with pictures of the High Line in it, a presentation piece.

My thought was to do it cheaply. Robert said, "It has to be fancy and expensive-looking. Then people will think that we are more than just two guys working out of our apartments." That would never have occurred to me. Phil Aarons said, "Listen, guys, if we can't raise enough money to print a brochure, we're never going to be able to raise enough money to do the High Line. You have to figure out how to do this."

An editor I knew got us Deb Wood, a graphic designer at Princeton Architectural Press. We collected the best photos we could find, and we laid out and printed this brochure. It was going to cost us $5,000, which seemed like a lot of money.

I called up Elizabeth Gilmore, a Greenwich Village resident who had expressed interest in supporting us in the past. Elizabeth had originally tracked down my phone number a few months earlier, after reading the article in *The Villager*. She had said she wanted to give us money. At that point, I said, "Well, that's great, but I don't think I can take your money. We're not set up for it." It's hard to imagine now that I would ever turn down money, but that's how new and young we were.

Elizabeth agreed to meet me for coffee at French Roast on Sixth Avenue. Even though she'd offered money before, I found it hard to ask for $5,000. She said, "I'll give you half." It was our first check. The rest of it we cobbled together from smaller donations, from our friends and family.

ROBERT

The brochure introduced the High Line and its history. At that time there was nothing printed about its history, so this was valuable information. It said, "There's a program called railbanking that could make the High Line a park; it's our mission to do that. I hope you'll help." It had quotes from Paula Cooper, Richard Meier, Christine Quinn, Lynden Miller, and Congressman Jerry Nadler, who had fought for the High Line with Peter Obletz back in the 1980s. Joel Sternfeld gave us the first of his photos just as we were going to press.

It was our first real action. We got it done in the summer of 2000. It said, "We're official, we exist, this is what we're doing."

JOSH

We weren't the only ones interested in the High Line. There was a mysterious British lawyer who had done some real estate development in New York. His name was Lionel Kustow, and he spoke in secretive terms about what he wanted to do with the High Line. CSX liked him, and Debra Frank was always trying to push us together. So Phil, Robert, and I went to lunch with Lionel at Aquavit, which was near MoMA, on Fifty-fourth Street.

ROBERT

Lionel wanted to use the High Line for a tourist train that went from Times Square down to the Meatpacking District. This was his big, secret idea. He said he had Virgin Atlantic as an investor. Phil and Lionel started talking about how there could be all different kinds of development along the High Line, and Josh became more and more incensed. He was pretty anti-development.

JOSH

Phil said that historic sites are usually threatened because a developer wants to build something bigger on the site. But zoning mechanisms could allow you to move the development rights above historic buildings to other sites, relieving the real estate pressure. That's how the City, spurred on by Jackie Onassis and MAS, saved Grand Central Terminal. The development rights above Grand Central were allowed to be sold to other locations. A similar mechanism was used to save the historic theaters in Times Square. If you did the same in the case of the High Line, it would mean property owners under the High Line would be given the ability to sell the development rights above the High Line to other properties in the neighborhood, which could lead to taller buildings on those receiving sites. It's an oversimplification, but it's the same end that Ed Kirkland had talked about. If the High Line was going to be saved, the development rights over the High Line were going to have to land somewhere. And wherever they landed, you would have taller buildings.

I had been sufficiently indoctrinated in the community dogma that tall buildings were the greatest evil you could possibly have, so I reacted very negatively to this notion. I said, "If the result of doing the High Line is that you end up with all these tall buildings that you wouldn't have had otherwise, I don't want to be part of it."

Phil told me that I would have to think about that, because it was the only way it could play out. Robert and I rode the subway back downtown together, and we had our first genuine fight.

ROBERT

Josh said, "Look, if you're going to work with these developers, I'm out of here. You can keep going, but I'm not going to help you anymore." We almost parted ways.

JOSH

I took me a while to move past this. At first I think I just denied it and told myself there was a different way it could turn out. Then, over time, my perspective changed. But it was certainly a major issue for me. Phil was describing a future that I couldn't see myself as part of.

ROBERT

Josh and I had talked in very broad terms about opening the High Line to the public, making it into a park, but we weren't architects, we weren't planners, and we didn't have an articulated vision for it. That turned out to be a key to the success of the project. We had to ask a lot of people to help us.

JOSH

The Design Trust for Public Space was an organization that described itself as the intersection between the design world, the government world, and the community world—three circles that were involved in making public spaces in New York City but that didn't interact well. It was the Design Trust's mission to bring those circles together for the common good. The trust was headed by Andrea Woodner and Claire Weisz. Andrea was also chair of the board, and the trust's founder. Phil suggested that we apply for one of its fellowships.

A community group was usually the applicant. The Design Trust would connect the group with design professionals and government advisers. The goal was to advance the community project at the City level, and at the same time instill it with a degree of design excellence that a community project might not normally pursue or have access to.

We got the fellowship, but they weren't giving us money. They were finding people to help us, and those people got the money. Everything was collaborative. Claire and Andy had super-charged brains. We would meet with them to frame out the project, and they were always full of new terms and ideas. I'd leave feeling intellectually nourished, but worried that we weren't going anywhere. It was the first time I heard the term *iterative process*. Architects love this term. I took "it's an iterative process" to mean that there would be many, many meetings and at each meeting we would undo what we decided in the previous meeting, and we would never really make a decision because, well, "it's an iterative process."

Eventually we resolved that we would do a planning study. If you look at the study now, it's remarkable how much it described what would happen in the years to come. It created a kind of road map for the High Line's transformation. But at that stage, what it meant was that Robert and I were thrown into a world of architects, planners, preservationists, landscape designers, and government people. It was a new world for me—

I fell in love with these people, with the way they thought and spoke, with everything that they were doing.

ROBERT
People think, oh, Giuliani must've hated the High Line. I don't think Giuliani cared at all about the High Line. Rather, the property owners who opposed the High Line had hired Randy Mastro, one of Giuliani's former deputy mayors, and paid him a lot of money to lobby Giuliani, and that's why Giuliani was opposed, in my view.

Phil orchestrated a meeting at City Hall to see if there was any chance of getting them to reconsider their pro-demolition policy. It was held in a room called the Crypt, underneath City Hall, a room with no windows. All these Giuliani officials came in—exactly the kind of big guys in suits you'd pull from central casting to play the deputies of an authoritarian, law-and-order mayor. After that meeting we knew we were never going to persuade Giuliani to change his mind. We were going to have to take legal action.

I used to think developers must be really smart: How else can they get their projects past opposition and build buildings people don't want? Now I've come to realize that not all developers are that smart. They just hire the smartest lawyers. But it can work the other way. You can hire the smartest lawyers to stop things from getting built or from being torn down. That's what we wanted to do.

We were looking at suing the railroad, the Surface Transportation Board, the City, the State, the property owners— all these entities at the same time. And we needed an expert in rail law. The firms that practice rail law usually represent a railroad, or the City, or the State as clients. None of them were that excited about suing entities that were usually their clients, and for free, and in a case that seemed so unlikely to go our way. There were lawyers who were willing to do it pro bono, but they weren't necessarily the best lawyers with the most applicable rail, State, or City experience, and we wanted to have the best. The government and the property owners would have the best lawyers on their side; we wanted the best on our side.

Richard Socarides started to help us around this time. He had been an adviser in the Clinton White House and knew a lot of people in Washington. Many rail lawyers are in Washington, because that's where the Surface Transportation Board is. Richard recommended Mike Hemmer, at Covington and Burling. We went and met with Mike in Washington. He was nice, and interested in the case, but didn't want to take it pro bono. I think he told us that it was going to cost $40,000. We had raised $5,000 before, to do the brochure, but now we had to raise $40,000. That's what generated our first fund-raiser.

We had to put it together very quickly. Get a bunch of people to give us their mailing lists. Print invitations. Mail them out. Robert did most of the work, because I was traveling for an article at the time.

ROBERT

The benefit was held in early December 2000. Olivia Douglas's assistant, Kelly, put all the lists together. We got Lucas Schoormans, a gallery owner in a building on West Twenty-sixth Street, to give us his space. Joel Sternfeld gave us a photograph to auction off. Gary Handel and an architect in Gary's firm, Ed Tachibana, created lots of photo boards and turned one of the gallery rooms into an exhibit about the High Line. James LaForce, a PR guy, helped get the word out. He got the event onto Page Six of the *Post*. Scott Skey, my boyfriend from college, did the catering. He was working at Caviar Russe at the time and got them to donate a bunch of caviar.

JOSH

At that point our great claim to stability was the PO box we had rented at the Old Chelsea Station post office on West Eighteenth Street. In the weeks after the invitations went out, I would open the mailbox and all these envelopes would pour out, full of checks. We charged $125 as the base ticket. I couldn't believe how many people wanted to give us $125. But there were also options to give more money, and suddenly I had checks in my hand for $500 and $1,000, and there was one check for $5,000. I thought, "Who are these people?"

ROBERT

That was the first time we understood that the donors would not necessarily be people we knew, that the way to raise money was to get in touch with friends of friends of friends. Take Donald Pels and Wendy Keys. They were friends of the parents of Will Sahlman, one of my friends. They didn't know us or anything about the project. They lived on the Upper East Side, and came all the way down to Chelsea for the benefit. They just thought it was interesting. Since that time, they've become two of our most loyal and generous supporters.

JOSH

Lucas Schoormans's gallery was in the West Chelsea Arts Building, on Twenty-sixth Street. When you got off the elevator, just before you went into the gallery, there was a big window with a great view northward, up the High Line.

It was the first time I'd ever met Bronson Van Wyck, who was an events designer and later became a member of our board. That night he'd rented a cherry picker with lights that shone down on that stretch of the High Line. It was very dramatic.

This was our first event, but it was already being done with fairly high production values: Bronson's lights, the beautiful foldout invitation with Joel's photography, which included a shot of the High Line from each season. Scott did these beautiful hors d'oeuvres and arranged for donated Piper-Heidsieck champagne. It was a fancy party for a fledgling organization.

Sandra Bernhard came, and Kevin Bacon and Kyra Sedgwick, because they had been on a friend's mailing list. Someone from the *Post* was there: Lois Weiss, the real estate reporter. So there was an article in the *Post* the next day about us, with a photo of Kevin and Kyra, with a headline that called the event a "Celeb Push" to save the High Line. It branded us as a celebrity project from this early point. This had a lot of advantages for us, though at certain times it brought us criticism. Mostly it has been an advantage.

ROBERT

The fund-raiser brought in $60,000, which allowed us to pay Mike Hemmer to prepare for our lawsuit, but then we didn't file it. This first lawsuit wasn't the right lawsuit at the right time. After that, Mike Hemmer started working for us pro bono, and he prepared many other filings for us for the Surface Transportation Board over the next few years. And eventually we filed a different lawsuit, a local, New York City lawsuit, and had to raise money for a different set of lawyers.

Even though we didn't file that first suit, it was an important thing for us to raise the money for it. When people donated, they got more involved and felt more committed. It forced us to create an infrastructure, build a database, and do the final push to file for 501(c)(3) status, the IRS designation for a nonprofit. At the time, we were still using the Municipal Art Society for tax purposes and allowing people to donate through them.

JOSH

In the early stages of fund-raising, the money is almost a secondary benefit. What you are getting is a group of people who have literally bought into your mission. That bonding—especially to a young, new organization—is a statement of partnership, or commitment, or belonging, or family, that is irreplaceable in any other way.

I recently dug out the program from that first event. It is remarkable how many people who came that night have been with us ever since.

Strategy Session

JOSH

At the start of 2001, we started looking down the road to the next mayor: Giuliani was going to term-limit out. A field of candidates was running to replace him, including Peter Vallone, the Council speaker, Fernando "Freddy" Ferrer, the Bronx borough president, and Mark Green, the public advocate. We needed to get all the candidates on board, since you couldn't know which one would win—though many expected that Green would.

Chris Collins reached out to us around this time. Chris was the City Council's zoning and land use counsel. Gifford Miller had introduced him to the High Line, asking if the City Council's approval was required for demolition. Chris lived in London Terrace with his partner, Bob Kulikowski, who worked for the Manhattan borough president, C. Virginia Fields.

Chris and Bob were instant converts. The first time they walked on the High Line, they got it. With their extensive experience in government and community work, they thought they could help, and proposed a strategy session. Chris invited us to their apartment for brunch.

Chris and Bob had set a table with food and wine by a window that overlooked Ninth Avenue. They showed me their bathroom, which they'd renovated in a style that was respectful of the 1930s style of London Terrace, the full-block apartment building that had become a neighborhood landmark.

The group was Chris, Bob, Robert, me, Phil Aarons, Gifford Miller, Richard Socarides, Mario Palumbo, Peter Rider from Christine Quinn's staff, and Brenda Levin, a close friend of Chris's and Bob's who had served on the planning commission for almost ten years. She had bright red hair and was skeptical of the High Line. Also there was Richard Emery, a highly regarded litigator and expert on City affairs.

Sitting in a circle in Chris and Bob's living room, we brainstormed, and a lot of the ideas that would carry us through the next few years took shape. I say "we," but it was not so much Robert and me as the others. They talked about winning over the City Council first. We had Gifford, we had Christine Quinn, and Bob could get the borough president. If we could turn all that into a supportive resolution from the entire City Council, we would have one side of City Hall—not as strong as the mayor, but something.

We had to hold off demolition until the next mayor took office. The idea of a City-based legal suit, instead of a federal suit around railroad issues, began to be fleshed out. Chris and Phil and Richard helped us zero in on the idea that the City charter governed land use decisions, which meant the City Council—not the mayor alone—had to approve certain actions.

We ended brunch having decided to seek a broad-based City Council resolution supporting adaptive reuse of the High Line while pursuing a legal strategy to block demolition at the same time.

It was Super Bowl Sunday. The meeting ended because there were a couple of people there who wanted to watch the game.

ROBERT

Phil told me I should connect with Amanda Burden. I didn't know who Amanda Burden was. He said, "She's on the City Planning Commission and is involved with the Municipal Art Society and Creative Time and a lot of civic organizations. She is as beautiful as she is talented, and very civic-minded." I looked her up and learned that she was also the daughter of a famous New York socialite, Babe Paley. She seemed very well connected.

So I called her and left a message. She called right back and said she would love to see the High Line. It was winter. We agreed to meet, but she didn't show. I figured, oh, she's too busy. It turned out I'd given her the wrong address. She'd been standing in the snow for almost an hour waiting for me. I thought she would never come back, but I set up another tour, and she came. Afterward we sat down at one of those tables in the concourse at Chelsea Market. I pulled out a map, and she started drawing on it. She had been appointed to the Planning Commission by Mark Green. But Giuliani actually ran the commission—the mayor appoints the majority of the commissioners and the chair. So Amanda wouldn't be able to do a lot for us. But she understood how saving the High Line could happen from a city planning and zoning standpoint. She got it.

JOSH

The Design Trust set up interviews with architects who could help us do the planning study. We agreed on Casey Jones and Keller Easterling. Casey would do the traditional planning study, and Keller would do an Internet-based planning project.

Casey started on the historical research—he was the one who tracked down a lot of those great old black-and-white photos you see in our literature. He did physical research, too. People would ask, "How big is the High Line?" And we had no idea. Casey had an architect's way of measuring things. He'd go up to the High Line and hang strings over the edge until they hit the ground, and then measure the strings. He did the first column studies and used computer-aided design software, or CAD, to bring them into the standard form used by architects. We used those CAD drawings for years.

He also did interviews. He would go to a group of transportation people and ask, "Is there a transportation future for the High Line?" He'd go to cycling groups and ask, "Is there a cycling future for the High Line?" He made land use maps in different colors, manufacturing here and residential there. It was an immersion course in all the subjects you have to start thinking about when you are doing a project like this.

At that time, I was still a writer for fluffy magazines, looking for hot trends and stylish new ways for readers to spend money. But I was also now in this amazing group of creative, dedicated architects, preservationists, planners, and parks advocates. Some meetings were torturously long and unproductive, but I would come away excited because of the people I was having the torturously long and unproductive meetings with.

ROBERT

Dirk McCall, someone I knew through another nonprofit, called me up and said, "My boss wants to meet you. He has an idea for the High Line. His name is Jim Capalino."

I did some research on Jim and found out he was a lobbyist for developers. I was skeptical. Why would a guy who represents developers be coming to help us out? But Jim knew Phil. The two had served together under Mayor Koch. So we met. He said, "I really want to get involved." At first I wondered if he was secretly representing the property owners who wanted to tear the High Line down, but we found he could be incredibly helpful. It was like with the lawyers: developers often hire the best lawyers, and they also hire the best lobbyists. Jim was a great lobbyist. At one of our bigger meetings, we were going around the room introducing ourselves, and he said, "I'm a fixer." Anytime I needed help, I would call Jim. If he didn't know the answer, he always knew who would. He would put me on hold, get that person on the phone, and conference us together, saying, "This is Robert Hammond. He's doing a great project. Help him out." He did that over and over.

JOSH

There was a panel in Midtown, where speakers were scheduled to talk about the West Side Rail Yards. Giuliani's original plan had been for the new Yankee Stadium to go on the rail yards, but there was huge opposition to that. Then the focus shifted toward the 2012 Olympics and a new stadium to bolster New York's bid against London and other cities.

Phil or Jim had told us we had to go to this meeting and stand up and say something, to insert the High Line into public discussion. Robert was supposed to speak, but the presentation went on and on, and Robert had a date, so he left. I had not been expecting to speak, and I was nervous. The room was filled with lawyers and City government people and developers. Joe Rose, the chair of the City Planning Commission, was at the podium. He'd said some critical things about the High Line in the press, so when the question-and-answer period came, I got up and asked my dutiful, terrified question: "The High Line is an elevated rail structure on the West Side; it actually goes into the rail yards. It offers all these opportunities. Don't you think we should be supporting this vision for reuse of the High Line?" Joe Rose responded with something along the lines of "I've seen that nice-looking brochure you guys made. You know how to make a nice brochure, but we need to focus on things that can actually get done."

ROBERT

We had presented at the community board and it hadn't gone so well, and we wanted to have a more positive meeting of our own. The Kitchen agreed to host it. The Kitchen is next to the High Line, on Nineteenth Street. The building is an old icehouse. It used to hold the blocks of ice that got shipped down the river. It had thick brick walls, painted black, with no windows.

Josh put up flyers. I sent out a lot of e-mails. We got a pretty good crowd.

Doug Oliver came. He said he owned a warehouse next to the High Line, between Twenty-fifth and Twenty-sixth streets, and he didn't want the High Line torn down because demolition would damage his building. Doug was the first big property owner along the Line who was supportive.

There was also a couple who lived in the neighborhood, Mike and Sukey Novogratz, who saw one of our flyers and were interested in our idea. After we explained the challenges we faced, they thought the project was unlikely. They signed their name to our supporter list but didn't get all that involved. Years later, though, they came back to us and were very generous. They helped pay to build one of the High Line's most popular features, the Tenth Avenue Square.

JOSH

The City Council's High Line hearing was scheduled for April. There was a lot riding on it. Christine and Gifford sponsored it. They stuck out their necks for us, and our part of the deal was to deliver a packed room.

We did our first comprehensive outreach to civic, community, and business groups for the hearing. We needed bodies, and we spent a lot of time on the phone, giving people sample text they could use in letters, collecting the letters, and begging people to come down to City Hall. It's a big ask to get people to come to City Hall. It pretty much kills the day.

In the process, we lined up the core group of institutional, community, and business supporters who have been with us ever since. The Municipal Art Society, the American Institute of Architects, the Architectural League, the Alliance for the Arts, and the American Planning Association, among many others. Jeff Ciabotti from the Rails-to-Trails Conservancy traveled from

Washington to testify. We even got a couple of the gallery people to attend—it's hard to get them to come to things outside the art world. Paula Cooper's assistant, Ona, came and sat there all day waiting to speak.

On the morning of the hearing, the *Daily News* ran an editorial that was supportive of our efforts. It was the first really positive press we'd ever had, and we took copies with us to pass out at the hearing.

The Council Chamber is a huge, old room with high ceilings, ornately painted. It's since been renovated, but at the time it was in a fairly advanced state of decay. The council members sat up on tiered rows at the front. The property owners, the railroad, and the mayor's people testified first. Then it was our turn. We testified in groups of two or three, sitting at a long table. The first panel comprised Olivia Douglas, Robert, and me. There was a ticking timer. As you were speaking, you saw it ticking down. At the beginning, one of the property owners said, "If you were actually able to make a park on the High Line, it would be great for property values. But this will never happen; it is just too far-fetched. These people are dreamers," he said. "It's a pipe dream."

Later in the afternoon, Amanda Burden testified at a table with Lynden Miller. She said, "Since when is being a dreamer a bad thing? This is a city that is built on dreams. We should all be following dreams like this one."

ROBERT

Joel's High Line photos, shot in all four seasons, were amazing. He had contacts at *The New York Times Magazine* and *The New Yorker*, and the photo editors at both wanted to run them.

At first we were going to go with *The New York Times Magazine*. But it turned out that Adam Gopnik had met Joel, had become interested in what Joel was doing, and wanted to write about it. With the prospect of Joel's photos being featured alongside a piece by Adam Gopnik, we gave the photos to *The New Yorker*.

People remember Adam's article as being about the High Line, but it was really about Joel and his process. It mentions Josh and me and our efforts—it calls us a group of "West Side do-gooders." The article paints a pretty unlikely picture of the project. But what it does capture is Joel's love of the High Line and Joel's personality, which became a major part of the story.

I think of Joel as a third cofounder. The photos he took became important tools for us. Instead of showing people architectural renderings, we would show Joel's photos. People could read different things into them. In one of his most famous photos of the High Line, looking east along Thirtieth Street on the rail yards section, you can see the Empire State Building, an old metal railroad box, the tracks, the various plants, and lots of different buildings, old and new. Some people would look at the photo and see a preservation project. Some would see horticulture. Rail buffs would get excited about the tracks. Some people imagined architecture. They would see say, "Look, there's the Empire State Building. This is right in the middle of Manhattan. You can build something up there."

JOSH

After the *New Yorker* article, people who hadn't heard of us before started to seek us out, but they had a hard time finding us. The voice mail number on our stationery wasn't listed, because you couldn't connect those cheap voice mail services to directory assistance.

One day I was at my computer working—we still worked in our home offices then—and the phone rang. The voice on the other end said, "Hi, my name is Edward Norton. I'm looking for the guys who are working on the High Line."

I thought, it's some other Edward Norton. It must be a common name. But as we kept talking, I said, "I'm sorry, but I have to ask . . . ?" And he said, "Yes, I'm that one."

Edward hadn't been able to find us after reading the *New Yorker* article, so he had called the Rail-to-Trails Conservancy, where his father had been a founding board member and had helped create the original railbanking legislation. He said, "Do you know these guys? I'm trying to reach them." Edward's grandfather was James Rouse, a developer and urban planner known for creating planned communities and urban marketplaces like Faneuil Hall in Boston, so along with the railbanking knowledge he'd gotten from his father, Edward had an interest in urban planning, too. He told me he used to live in the West Coast building, on Horatio Street. He would hang out on the roof drinking beers and would look down on the High Line and wonder what would become of it.

ROBERT

Our first office space was at the Neighborhood Preservation Center, next to St. Mark's Church, in the East Village. They had small offices that new organizations could rent for six months or a year. It was at a time when there were a lot of Internet incubators. In this case, it was a nonprofit incubator. It was great for us, because we didn't have enough money to pay regular office rent.

We hired Dahlia Elsayed part time. She was an artist who had worked with me at the catalog company and the HIV/AIDS website. She helped us with letters, basic accounting, and getting ready for events.

Our space was in the basement. It had no windows and was big enough to fit only a desk and one filing cabinet. It was impossible for all three of us to be there at the same time. Josh and I were still mostly working from home.

JOSH

Christine Quinn's chief of staff, Peter Rider, came on a tour of the High Line, and as we were walking up there, he said, "You should think about joining the community board. The borough president makes the appointments, but Christine, as the local council member, gets to recommend people. It might be a good thing for the project. You'd be more plugged in."

I was still traveling a lot, and when you join the community board you're committing to three or four nights a month. But I decided to give it a shot. I filled out the paperwork, interviewed at the borough president's office, and was appointed. The first meeting of the full board that I attended as a member was in June. Now I was on the other side of the big U-shaped table. There was a controversial nightclub proposal on the agenda, and the meeting went almost until midnight. I'd never seen the long period of arguing and voting that takes place at the end of those meetings, which can carry you into the wee hours—all bright fluorescent lights and linoleum and people perfectly happy to stay forever and talk and talk and talk. A few of my fellow community board members seemed a little nuts. I came home and said to Stephen, "Oh, my God, what have I done?"

ROBERT

The Design Trust held a panel discussion called "The Future of the High Line." We had spent months planning it over breakfasts at French Roast with Andy, Claire, Casey, and Alex Washburn, an architect who had worked with Senator Moynihan. The idea was to broaden and elevate the discussion. Marilyn Jordan Taylor, head of Skidmore, Owings and Merrill, and Charles Shorter, from Ernst & Young, were featured speakers. The panel was held in the offices of the Port Authority, on the sixty-seventh floor of the World Trade Center.

JOSH

At the same time, we were preparing a lawsuit against the City and needed to raise funds for that. Our next fund-raiser was going to be a combined art auction, cocktail party, and dinner. Phil Aarons asked Mary Boone to host us in her gallery.

We hired a consultant, Doug Wingo, to help manage the event and the auction. We wanted some of the auction pieces to be High Line related, so we brought artists on tours. Joel donated a photo. Tom Sachs trespassed on the High Line and made a piece about that. Christo and Jeanne-Claude gave us a piece. Jeanne-Claude called Robert and scolded him because we'd sent them a two-page letter printed on two pages instead of on both sides of the same page.

We scheduled the event for mid-July, the Siberia of New York City's social calendar. But our support base was young, they worked, they didn't go to the Hamptons all summer. We had that part of the calendar pretty much to ourselves.

ROBERT

I hoodwinked Amanda Burden and Alex von Furstenberg into chairing the event at Mary Boone's. I said, "Will you play a role?" Amanda said yes, and then I made her a co-chair, which I don't think she knew she had signed up for. But she was gracious about it. It gave us credibility to have someone so involved in civic life get on board. I did the same thing with Alex. "Will you help?" Then I made him a co-chair.

Alex was introduced to me by Florent Morellet, of the restaurant Florent. Florent was working on a preservation project in the Meatpacking District that Alex's mother, Diane von Furstenberg, supported. We met for the first time at Alex's office on West Twelfth Street. He was just so handsome and friendly, and he had an amazing body; he'd parked his motorcycle under the office stairs. Alex's father was a prince, Prince Egon von Furstenberg, and so Alex was a prince, too. You have this idea of what a prince should be, but usually you're disappointed. Alex looked and acted like a true storybook prince.

JOSH

Bill Cunningham came from the *Times* and photographed at Mary Boone's. The next Sunday we were in the party pages.

You could feel the organization ramping up. After cocktails and the auction, we went to dinner at The Park restaurant, which was brand new. It was a beautiful summer night. We were on an open-air deck above the restaurant. Bronson put flowers and candles everywhere and beamed lights across Tenth Avenue to light up the High Line. Robert had seated me next to Diane von Furstenberg, the beautiful, elegant designer whom, until then, I'd only ever read about in magazines. I didn't really know what to say to her. It was one of those nights of feeling, Oh my, I've entered a whole new world.

ROBERT

Some of my straight friends who came to our early events would say, "Wow, there are a lot of men here." Josh and I are gay, and a lot of our friends are gay, so a disproportionate number of our early supporters were gay men. Not just because of Josh and me, but also because the High Line runs through two famously gay neighborhoods, Chelsea and the West Village.

People would pretend that they discovered the High Line when they were going to art galleries, but it was really when they were going to gay dance parties at Twilo, the Tunnel, or the Roxy.

Gayness ultimately became an identifying characteristic of the organization and, to some degree, of the park itself.

Demolition?

ROBERT

The federal lawsuit was still on hold, but the City lawsuit was moving forward. We had hired Richard Emery, who was famous for a 1989 lawsuit that fundamentally changed the governmental structure of New York City. His suit had challenged the Board of Estimate, which had power over budget and land use decisions, because the city's most populous borough, Brooklyn, had no more voting power than its least populous borough, Staten Island. Because of that suit, the City Charter was rewritten in 1990, and the Board of Estimate's powers were given to the City Council.

John Cuti, one of Richard's partners, managed our case. The suit we were filing was called an Article 78 challenge. It basically said that for the City to participate in the demolition of the High Line, it had to take the matter through Uniform Land Use Review Procedure, or ULURP, which is a nine-month review process to bring land use decisions past the community board, the borough president, the Department of City Planning, and then to the City Council.

JOSH

The property owners were speeding things up because the Giuliani administration's term was ending and they wanted to get the deal done first. This made us work faster, too. And the faster we worked, the more they knew they were up against something real. They began to work even faster to get the demolition papers in order. Our work to save the High Line seemed to be accelerating their efforts to tear it down.

We would meet at Richard Emery's office up on Madison Avenue. I'd never spent much time around there, behind St. Patrick's, by the Palace Hotel. Now I was there all the time.

Usually it was Chris, Phil, Robert, Mario, and me, hashing through the case and reading drafts that John Cuti and his associate Ilann Maazel had drafted. We had to sign up six neighborhood plaintiffs. We wanted it to be a broad, community-based suit, not just Friends of the High Line. I was in charge of getting other people in the community to join us in suing the City.

Paula Cooper didn't need much convincing. A neighbor, Rodney Durso, also joined—he'd come to our first, disastrous, community board hearing and reached out to us afterward to offer support. Zazel Loven, who's head of my local block association, agreed, too. Mark Kingsley, the board chair of a condo building near the High Line, signed on, along with Sara Fitzmaurice, who ran a public relations firm in the neighborhood—Sara's firm represented Dia Center for the Arts. The sixth community plaintiff was Rowann Gilman, a High Line volunteer I often saw at the dog park.

ROBERT

The Manhattan borough president, C. Virginia Fields, and the City Council joined the challenge. The Council also helped us pay the legal fees, because Gifford and Chris Collins were able to convince Speaker Peter Vallone that an important Council prerogative was at stake. The City Council had only had power over land use matters for ten years at that point, and Peter Vallone was supportive of protecting that power.

We used two arguments to support our case that the City's decision to demolish had to go through ULURP. One, it was an acquisition of real property. In the transfer of parts of the structure and its easement back to the city just before demolition, the City would be acquiring "real property," and the City needs to go through ULURP before acquiring "real property."

The other was that the High Line was on the City Map, an official record that shows streets, parks, public places, and easements. Removing the High Line would change the City map, and this would, by law, require ULURP. Chris and Bob, from their years of work for the City, knew that each borough had an obscure employee, the borough engineer, whose job included keeping the documents that made up the City Map. In the case of Manhattan, that person was Tony Gulotta, who had retired, but Chris and Bob tracked him down. Not only did he know the High Line, but he supported our argument. The City Law Department, meanwhile, got a legal expert to argue that the High Line was on the City Map only for "informational purposes."

JOSH

A preservation group called Landmark West, based on the Upper West Side, held a series of breakfasts with all the mayoral candidates. You paid twenty dollars and you got your coffee and your bagel, and you got to hear the candidate talk about preservation issues. Jim and Chris told us we needed to go to each breakfast and ask a question about the High Line and get each candidate to say that he supported the High Line, to make it one of his promises.

I did two of them: the Freddy Ferrer breakfast at the Saloon, near Lincoln Center, and the Mike Bloomberg breakfast, at the Empire Hotel.

Before the Bloomberg breakfast, I had to write my question down on a piece of paper and go hide in a stall in the bathroom and read it to myself over and over to build up my courage.

Bloomberg did his speech, and I stood up and asked my question: As you may know, Mr. Bloomberg, the High Line is an elevated rail structure on the West Side, and we think it offers this unique opportunity to blah, blah, blah, and would you be supportive of an effort like that?

He said, "Yes, it's a no-brainer."

Following those breakfasts, we went back to each campaign and asked the candidate to sign a letter to the head of CSX saying, "I'm running for mayor of New York, and I support the High Line, so please don't take any action that will threaten it." They all did. Robert knew Jonathan Capehart, who was part of the Bloomberg campaign. Jonathan told Robert the campaign was working on a white paper defining Bloomberg's policy on parks. If we got information to Jonathan, he could make sure that the High Line was referenced in it. So we did that, and when they posted the white paper on their campaign website, it had the High Line in it. The High Line was part of the grand vision for parks in New York City for candidate Bloomberg.

Not that we thought Bloomberg would be mayor. It was pretty much expected that the next mayor was going to be Mark Green. There was a lot of excitement in our camp about Green, because if he was elected, then it was likely that Amanda Burden would become the new chair of the Planning Commission. Plus, as public advocate he had been the first City official to support the project. Allen Roskoff, a City activist whom Robert knew, had introduced him to us.

ROBERT

Joel convinced his gallery at the time, Pace/MacGill, that it was important to show his High Line photos immediately, because Mayor Giuliani was mobilizing to tear the High Line down. At the same time, he got a German art publisher to publish a book called *Walking the High Line*, with a selection of the photographs and a reprint of Adam Gopnik's *New Yorker* piece. He got them to rush everything. It was such a tight time line that Gerhard Steidl, the publisher, had to have a Lufthansa flight held at the airport in Germany so he could get a box of books on it to make it for the opening of Joel's show at Pace/MacGill; we'd invited our supporters there for a signing. The box arrived at JFK at 5:00 p.m., one hour before the signing.

JOSH

Casey Jones had been paid to do the Design Trust study for a period of eight or nine months. We were supposed to end up with a book, but his time and money ran out after the research period.

Some text had been drafted, jammed with information. I jumped in to write the final version, and began pumping out text.

We set up a conference call to review where the text stood. Casey Jones and Karen Hock—Karen was managing the project for the Design Trust—were just starting the call when I got an e-mail from Stephen from work, telling me to turn on the TV. The news was still showing the early footage, smoke coming from just one tower. We kept talking, but the images kept coming. I was seeing them out of the corner of my eye. I don't remember exactly which image made me say, "Listen, guys, I think we need to end this call. Something intense is going on."

ROBERT

I was at my apartment, trying to get on the conference call, and someone said, "Well, the call is canceled: a plane just went into the World Trade Center." I said, "Then let's reschedule it for eleven thirty," and I went up on my roof to see what had happened.

Embarrassingly and selfishly, my first thought when I realized the towers had fallen was, Well, there goes the High Line. Who's going to ever care about the High Line when we have a disaster on this scale?

JOSH

There was a moment after 9/11 when people had to decide if they were going to stay in the city. Was it naïve to stay? Stephen and I were about to buy our apartment and gut it. Did we still want to do that? The High Line just vanished from our lives for a while. Then we had to come back and figure out what to do with this thing we had started.

People thought that New York could never go back to a state that could be called normal. Our group had a lot of searching discussions about the High Line. Many were in the context of the Design Trust study, because that was the most pressing deadline. The first e-mail newsletter after 9/11 was on October 18. It took us from September 11 to October 18 to cobble together a position on why the High Line was still relevant.

We said we were committed to the future of New York City, this was a future-oriented project, and this was not the time to be tearing things down. That was actually a big point for us. The demolition of the High Line was going to be very destructive, the ground was going to shake, it was going to be dusty and noisy. People were not up for anything that disruptive. But greater than that was that the High Line was about New York moving forward.

ROBERT

People wanted to do something for New York, and they didn't know how to help at Ground Zero. They couldn't rebuild the

World Trade Center themselves. The High Line was something positive they could work on, something that wasn't so weighted with emotion.

As a result of 9/11, average people got engaged in things that previously only architects and planners had cared about. Design competitions and architectural renderings were on the front page of the *Post* regularly. It became commonplace for people to say things like "Should we reestablish the street grid through the super-block?" There was a huge forum held at the Javits Center for Ground Zero planning, and thousands of people went. The High Line fit into that.

One scary thing after 9/11 was the idea that Mayor Giuliani might stay in office, that he would somehow extend his term. Amanda Burden was campaigning for Mark Green for mayor. I voted for Green. A lot of friends were working for him, and we figured some of them might end up in his administration, in addition to Amanda.

My friend Jonathan Capehart was working for Bloomberg, and Bloomberg was supporting us, too. Before 9/11, Bloomberg was thought to be a long shot. But after 9/11, everything changed. He won. The year before, Bush had won, and now another Republican had won. Even though Bloomberg had been supportive as a candidate, we didn't know what his ultimate position on the High Line would be. And Amanda would not be the planning chair.

JOSH

After nearly a year working on the Article 78 suit, we filed our legal papers in December. The Giuliani administration was in its final days, and we thought he would try to sign the demolition papers before he left office. I was in St. John with Stephen, staying in an eco-tent compound called Maho Bay, where there were no TVs or phones. I would call in to Robert twice a day from a payphone to find out what was going on. Things started moving really fast just before Christmas.

ROBERT

First we got a temporary restraining order. That stopped the City from signing the demolition papers until a hearing could take place in January. We sent out an e-mail update to all our supporters, calling it a victory.

The next day the City appealed, and the appellate judge vacated the temporary restraining order, which meant there was nothing to stop the City from committing to demolition.

Then, just days before leaving office, the Giuliani administration signed the demolition papers. It was a big setback. A new mayor can't just overturn a commitment made by a previous mayor. Giuliani himself hadn't been able to undo the ninety-nine-year lease Mayor Dinkins had signed with the U.S. Tennis Association in his final days, allowing the expansion of the U.S. Open courts onto City parkland. Bloomberg was more supportive of the High Line than Giuliani, but we were going into the new administration with the City having signed the papers. That was the first time that I thought, wow, look out for the bulldozers.

JOSH

When Robert told me that the papers had been signed, I stood there at the payphone in St. John with this sinking feeling.

I had come to the High Line with a fairly simplistic view of a save-the-anything kind of fight: a lot of yelling and screaming, and then the famed chaining yourself to the thing so that a bulldozer can't tear it down. Part of me originally thought that's what saving the High Line was going to be about.

Early in the game, Phil helped us see that this was going to be a different kind of process. But I always worried about the bulldozers. Every time I left town, I thought that the High Line would be torn down while I was away.

The example I held in my mind was the Thunderbolt, in Coney Island. It was a twin rollercoaster to the Cyclone, but there had been a fire on it, so it stopped running. It stood there by the beach, covered with vines, and it still had the great, old Thunderbolt sign. People wanted to save the Thunderbolt, but the City tore it down before anyone could mobilize. Giuliani had plans for a minor-league baseball stadium there.

That's what will happen to the High Line, I often thought.

ROBERT

Lynden Miller called me up and said, "I saw a crane going up near the High Line." It's the only time I really thought, okay, we're going to need to use the e-mail list to mobilize people to sit in front of bulldozers. I never wanted this to be an organization that had to resort to that. But we would have been out there. I always relished the idea of Amanda Burden chained to the High Line. I think she would have been happy to chain herself to it.

At City Hall

ROBERT

In January 2002, Gifford Miller was elected speaker of the City Council, the second most powerful position in New York City government. I had supported him in his campaign, as he built support with the other council members—but it had seemed like a long shot. People said, "You'll never have a white speaker from Manhattan. You'll never have someone that young." At thirty-two, Gifford would be the youngest speaker ever.

JOSH

We had been excited to think that the Mayor's Office might go back to the Democrats, after eight years of Giuliani. You could make the distinction that Bloomberg wasn't a "true" Republican, that he'd been a Democrat before. But he had won as a Republican, and the Democrats had lost. The chance for Amanda to be Mark Green's planning chair was lost, too.

Then the buzz began on our conference calls with Phil and Chris Collins and Jim Capalino: Bloomberg was talking to Amanda. I opened the Metro section of the *Times* one morning in January and there was a picture of Amanda coming down a back staircase at City Hall, and she was smiling. Bloomberg had made her his planning chair.

This was right on the heels of Gifford being elected speaker. Two people who had been strong supporters of the High Line from the start were suddenly in positions of influence, one on each side of City Hall—the council's side and the mayor's side.

ROBERT

Even though the Bloomberg administration was more favorable to the High Line than Giuliani's had been, Giuliani's people had signed the demolition papers, and we didn't know if Bloomberg could undo that commitment. So the Article 78 lawsuit had to go forward: we were still suing the City. The City wanted to pursue the case, too. It's in the interest of the City Law Office to preserve power and flexibility for the Mayor's Office, and if we prevailed, that power and flexibility would be slightly diminished, in that the Mayor's Office would be required to submit any similar future cases to ULURP. They didn't want it to create a precedent.

JOSH

I was trapped in my half-demolished, half-renovated apartment, surrounded by contractors, getting the Design Trust book finished. The idea was to make a document that would convince government officials that reusing the High Line was a great thing. It would also contain the basic information an architect or planner might need to start a master plan. And it would act as a public information piece.

We worked with Jonathan Capehart to turn the High Line bit from Bloomberg's white paper on parks into an introduction, and Bloomberg signed off on it. So the book would open with an introduction from the mayor and end with an essay from Betsy Barlow Rogers, who had cofounded the Central Park Conservancy.

ROBERT

Paula Scher at Pentagram designed the book. One of Joel's photos ran on the cover. Richard Socarides was working for

AOL–Time Warner, and he got them to pay for the printing. When you look at the book today, it's fascinating: a lot of what we outlined in it ended up happening. We presented the book to the public with an exhibition at the Municipal Art Society.

JOSH

Ed Tachibana worked for Gary Handel, and he translated the book into display boards for the exhibition. Ed, Dahlia, and I loaded the exhibition into MAS from a rented U-Haul parked on Madison Avenue—we didn't have money to pay people to do it. The boards were heavy, and hauling them up the marble stairs of the Villard Houses was a slog. I bitched about it to Robert afterward, because he had been out of town. I think he was down south, at a Radical Faeries retreat.

ROBERT

In the back of the Design Trust book we listed our supporters. The people at Edison Properties—the organizers of the Chelsea Property Owners group—looked up our supporters' addresses and periodically mailed each of them a flyer called "High Line Reality." On it, the letters in the word *Reality* were crumbling, to suggest that the High Line was in danger of falling down. Each flyer had a new theme. One showed a picture of the High Line in winter, looking very bleak, just weeds. In big letters, it read, "Money doesn't grow on trees, and last we checked it wasn't growing in the weeds of the High Line, either." The campaign made us nervous. We didn't have the resources or the time to counter these efforts.

JOSH

Amanda received the "High Line Reality" flyers, too. One mailing included a bit of old cement that had come off the High Line— the property owners were trying to prove that it was falling down. Amanda laughed and fluttered her hands as she described the scene this mailing created in her office at the City Planning Commission. Crumbling gray stuff coming out of an envelope could cause quite a commotion during this post-9/11 period, after an anthrax mailing had shut down the Senate.

ROBERT

While the Design Trust exhibition was up at MAS, the Preservation League of New York State named the High Line one of their annual "Seven to Save." It was the first time a statewide group recognized the High Line as a preservation priority. Eero Saarinen's TWA terminal at JFK was on the same list of seven. Most people still thought of the High Line as a rusty old pigeons' nest, so seeing it put in the same league as an iconic piece of architecture like the TWA building was a big advance for us.

A contact at the French consulate told us that the mayor of Paris, Bertrand Delanoë, was coming to New York, so we invited him to tour the High Line. Gifford went to greet him at the rail yards section at Thirty-fourth Street. We had to do it at the rail yards, because our access through Chelsea Market had been cut off—the Market was enclosing the old rail platform to rent it out as office space.

It gets windy at the rail yards, and it was one of those miserable days with what the weather people call a "wintry mix"—snow, rain, and hail all at the same time. Delanoë walked about fifty feet onto the rail yards section and then turned around and left.

Before the visit, his staff had been talking about giving the High Line a $100,000 grant—a gesture of support for New York after 9/11. After that visit, they stopped returning our calls.

ROBERT

Gifford was now speaker, and in one of his first meetings with the mayor, he identified the High Line as one of his top priorities. At the same time, Amanda started talking to Dan Doctoroff. Dan was Bloomberg's deputy mayor for economic development and was behind the City's 2012 Olympics bid. Amanda took Dan up on a tour of the High Line, which usually won people over, but she said it would take more work to convince him.

JOSH

Amanda and Gifford got us the chance to make a pitch to Dan during the first month of the new administration, which shows how hard they were pushing for it.

When you go up the stone steps to City Hall and inside the main hall, you can go right, to the council side, or left, to the mayor's side. Previously, I had always gone right, to the council side, where we had allies. This was the first time I turned left.

On the mayor's side, there are two wooden benches in front of a swinging gate. Generally you sit on these hard benches and wait for someone to bring you upstairs. Jim Capalino and Phil Aarons and Robert were already there waiting. Laurel Blatchford, who worked for Dan, eventually came down and brought us up into the open office Bloomberg had set up in the former Board of Estimate chamber. The newspapers had given this new arrangement a lot of attention. Instead of using the private mayoral office, Bloomberg had created a bullpen-style workplace, where he and everyone sat together in open cubicles and had access to lots of snacks supplied daily. He was bringing the culture of Bloomberg LP to City Hall, and updating City Hall technologically. Before Bloomberg, most City offices didn't have e-mail.

ROBERT

We met in a stately round room called the COW, for the Committee of the Whole. We were presenting the High Line from a planning perspective, and we used a lot of Joel's photographs, which had emotional power. Dan said, "Don't show me pretty pictures. We have so many parks already that we can't afford."

JOSH

Dan was a tall man with dark curly hair. He seemed sure of himself, and I was intimidated by him. He told us, "You're not telling me about the money. I need to know what this means financially."

Phil said, "That's fair. Will you give us the chance to come back to you with that part of the story?"

When we left, Jim Capalino took us across to the council side, to the Members' Lounge. He sat us down and said, "Let me tell you what Dan just said to you. Dan just said that you need to commission an economic feasibility study. And, respectfully, guys, you don't have a choice. If you don't do it, the High Line isn't going to happen. And I know whom you need to hire to do it: John Alschuler, who did Dan's economic feasibility study for the Olympics." He pulled out his phone, called Alschuler's office, and set up a meeting. When he hung up, he said, "This is going to cost you a lot of money. I know you don't have the money, but you are going to have to find it."

A pattern was establishing itself. The brochure, the legal fees, and now this study all took money that we didn't have. We could only repeat Phil's line about the brochure—one that we would repeat many times again in the future: If we can't raise the money for this, we'll never raise enough money to build the High Line.

ROBERT

We met with John Alschuler, and I thought, I want to hire this guy, because I found him so compelling. He had the ability to encapsulate complex concepts in simple terms. He figured out how to frame the argument in that first meeting: parks increase the value of nearby real estate, which leads to higher property taxes, and thus the addition of a new park on the High Line could create an economic benefit for New York City.

I wanted to learn from him. At that point I was not being paid, but I felt that my compensation was working with people I could learn from.

JOSH

John's firm was at Fifty-eighth and Broadway, a great old building with a gleaming marble lobby and elevators trimmed with brass. The offices had bare wood corridors, so there was a lot of clacking as his young staff moved around. John's office was in the corner, with windows looking out on Columbus Circle. The Time Warner Center was under construction. We watched it go up during our meetings with John that summer.

John was another striking new person to come to the project, with thick silver hair that looked expensively cut. He wasn't old enough to be my father, but he had a warm, fatherly way with us. John was good at talking people through things that they didn't understand. He quickly explained how this project would take shape.

ROBERT

John said, "How about if we answer this question: Over a twenty-year time period, will the High Line generate more direct revenues to the City from property taxes than it costs to build?" Even though the City was not going to pay for the whole thing—Friends of the High Line would help pay for it—we needed to establish that it was a good investment for the City.

JOSH

One of John's associates, Jon Meyers, did a district-wide assessment of existing property values and tax revenues. Then he and John projected what would happen to those property values with the addition of an attractive new park on the High Line. They couldn't give the park credit for increased property values that would be created by the rezoning of the neighborhood, because the rezoning would happen with or without the High Line. Rather, they calculated the value that would be added to properties only by the presence of the park. To do that, they looked at how other parks increased property values—not just Central Park, but also small New York City parks such as Duane Park, in Tribeca. It was predicted that value would come from three factors: proximity to the park, the extra window walls that would be created in buildings adjacent to the High Line, and the establishment of a marketable district identity. The identity of the High Line would rub off on the neighborhood, creating value beyond the edges of the park, as had happened with Gramercy Park in the nineteenth century.

ROBERT

The study ended up showing that the High Line would cost $65 million to build but would create some $140 million in incremental tax revenues for the City over a twenty-year period. This changed the way we thought of the project. It was larger than just a single park. We started actively trying to promote the idea of a High Line neighborhood, a High Line District.

John Alschuler knew that Dan would never support the High Line if it obstructed his plans for the Olympics, which included a stadium on the rail yards. So he brought in the engineering firm

Parsons Brinckerhoff to demonstrate the different ways you could reroute the High Line around a stadium while still meeting the requirements of the federal railbanking legislation, which required connectivity to the national rail system. Because trains need a lot of space to ramp up to a height of thirty feet and the stadium would eat into that space, some of the options were outlandish. One option showed an elevator to lift the trains up to the High Line. Another showed a cog railway, the same kind of system that pulled trains up steep mountains in the Swiss Alps. "We don't have to show that it's likely or logical," John said. "Just that it's possible."

JOSH

John was giving us a good rate, but this was going to be an expensive job. We called up Juliet Page and asked her if she had any ideas for funders. Juliet worked in development at New Yorkers for Parks, and she had already helped us get our first two foundation grants, one from the JM Kaplan Fund, the other from the Merck Family Fund. Juliet said this was a project that might interest the Greenacre Foundation, which she'd worked with in the past. So she called up Ruth Kuhlmann at Greenacre and convinced her to take a proposal to her board.

Greenacre gave us $50,000 for the study—the biggest grant we'd ever received. Juliet also talked us through how to ask our top donors to contribute. With her guidance, we asked Donald Pels and Wendy Keys to help. Donald and Wendy had come to our first benefit, in 2000. They lived on the Upper East Side, so the High Line would have no impact on their immediate community—Central Park and Carl Schurz Park were their neighborhood parks. Yet the High Line continued to interest them, and they decided to help us with funding the feasibility study.

ROBERT

Around this time, Jo Hamilton and Florent Morellet were trying to get the Meatpacking District designated as a historic district. Diane von Furstenberg supported the effort, which was called Save Gansevoort Market. Jo and Florent became great allies for us.

JOSH

Florent had opened the restaurant Florent in 1985. The place put the neighborhood on people's radar. You stepped through meat scraps and fatty slime on the sidewalk to this 1940s diner that Florent had lovingly restored, with Formica tables, a red leather banquette that ran the length of the room, and framed maps of cities. Florent had a staff that gave the impression of being club kids or performers or drag queens when they weren't waiting tables. The feeling was magical. It was democratic and welcoming—a great New York City scene.

Now Florent was working with Jo, a vivacious, stylish woman who lived on Jane Street, to keep what was special about the neighborhood from being lost.

ROBERT

Most historic districts have a visible historic style—colonial; or McKim, Mead and White—whereas the meat market was a collection of low-rise meatpacking buildings. They were not what people generally thought of as landmarks, but people in the neighborhood loved them. The Save Gansevoort Market project was similar to the High Line in this respect. It made people see the beauty of something that was not traditionally thought of as beautiful.

JOSH

The High Line and Save Gansevoort Market were both viewed as crazy causes that probably wouldn't succeed. Robert and I started meeting Florent and Jo at the restaurant. We felt like co-conspirators—the cinematic version of community organizing, the four of us tucked into a corner table at this funny downtown restaurant, scheming about who might be on our side at City Hall.

Florent always sat at the first table on the right, tucked into the corner. The waiters set his table with cloth napkins and would bring him that day's soup to taste. He was his own kind of New York celebrity, and being at his table made us feel cooler than we were.

Under the Fence Tour

ROBERT

In March 2002 the judge hearing our case ruled that it was unlawful for the City to have signed the demolition papers for the High Line without going through the land use review process—we'd won! We'd actively worked on this lawsuit for over a year—it had been central to our strategy—yet I don't remember what I felt or where I was when I got the good news. We didn't celebrate. That was typical. More than once we would make a big advance, but there would still be so much to do that we didn't stop to savor our little successes. A development director who worked with us later, Diane Nixa, said ours was the only office she'd ever worked in where you could get a million-dollar gift and everyone would just keep on working.

JOSH

A press release had to go out quickly, and it circulated endlessly among Phil, Chris Collins, Robert, me, and our lawyers, Richard Emery and John Cuti. We didn't get much press out of the verdict. The *Times* gave it five sentences in a Metro roundup. The ruling was a big deal to us, but it did not guarantee anything. The City was going to appeal, for sure, and we still had to win over Dan Doctoroff with our feasibility study, but for now, at least, the High Line wasn't coming down.

ROBERT

In April, the Mayor's Office hired Turner Construction to assess the structural integrity of the High Line, and announced that they would consider our economic feasibility study alongside Turner's assessment. When the Chelsea Property Owners got wind of this, they started doing a study of their own, showing the economic benefits that would come from tearing the High Line down. Their argument was that you'd get bigger, simpler, and more valuable building sites without the High Line there.

JOSH

Two community meetings took place that spring. One was a public hearing in April, held by Community Board 4. Community Board 2 had endorsed us, but Community Board 4, where most of the High Line was located, still hadn't taken a position on the issue. It was hard for us—we were presenting ourselves as a community project, and a local community board hadn't endorsed us. But with the list of neighbors and civic groups we'd developed at the City Council hearing, we brought twenty-five people to speak, and more to cheer them on. We got them there early, so they spoke at the start of the hearing, setting the tone.

Our study was based on the assumption that there would be future development in the neighborhood, and we wanted to get that fact out there at the beginning. So we set up a community meeting at the O. Henry School, on West Seventeenth Street, and John Alschuler presented some of the material of the feasibility study. This was the first meeting where including the High Line in a future rezoning was discussed explicitly. As expected, people were supportive of the High Line, but the subject of future development in the neighborhood put some people on edge.

ROBERT

We had to raise money to keep the doors open, to keep hiring lawyers and consultants, but Josh and I weren't being paid. I had kept doing consulting jobs to support myself, but I was spending most of my time on the High Line. I decided I wanted to start taking a salary.

I was very nervous about this. Many donors were my friends, and I felt uncomfortable asking for money if part of it would go toward paying me. Josh felt the same.

But I asked Phil and other board members about the idea,

and they were enthusiastic. They worried that Josh and I wouldn't keep doing the project if we weren't being paid. They thought it would ultimately be good for the High Line.

When I talk to people who are starting organizations, I see the same reluctance to pay themselves. They will pay for anything else. They would rather pay for office supplies.

But salaries made us a real organization. It is not a real organization until people are being paid. You can go only so far with just volunteers.

JOSH

John Cuti, one of the lawyers for our lawsuit, was Martha Stewart's son-in-law. He asked Martha if we could hold our summer benefit in her new space in the Starrett-Lehigh Building, on West Twenty-sixth Street. She said yes, and she also agreed to be an event chair. Starrett-Lehigh was a landmarked railroad warehouse that dated to the same period as the High Line, so there was a historic connection.

Edward Norton agreed to be an event chair, too. He wanted to see the High Line firsthand before he wrote his remarks, so we made a date to walk it. I hadn't met him before. We had only talked on the phone.

The sole access we had to the High Line then was at the rail yards. You entered though a gate at Thirty-fourth Street, across from the Javits Center. Laurie Izes from CSX waited there with me for Edward to arrive. Laurie had replaced Debra Frank as the railroad's representative. You couldn't go up on the High Line without her. She made you sign a waiver of liability and checked that you were wearing flat shoes. If someone was not wearing flat shoes, she would refuse to let them up. If an important socialite arrived in Manolos you couldn't just turn her away—or I couldn't. But Laurie could.

Edward was late. Part of me thought he wouldn't come. But then a yellow cab pulled up, and there he was.

Usually, when we went up from Thirty-fourth Street, we'd go as far as Twenty-ninth Street and turn back, because CSX had installed a steel fence at Twenty-ninth Street to keep trespassers from going south. But those same trespassers had dug the gravel away from under the corrugated steel panels and made a slot that you could shimmy under. You had to lie on your belly and pull yourself through the gravel, dirt, and broken glass. Once you were through, you could see the next part, from Twenty-ninth Street down to Fourteenth Street. We called this kind of visit an under-the-fence tour. You had to be skinny or it wouldn't work.

Edward's tour was an under-the-fence tour. He got on his belly and started going under. His torso made it, and then Laurie and I pretended not to look at his butt as he wriggled it through.

Edward told me later that he went back to the High Line shortly afterward—he trespassed and did the same walk again with Brad Pitt.

ROBERT

The dinner at Martha Stewart's space coincided with her legal troubles, which were in the papers every day. At the last minute, her attorneys recommended that she not appear at a big public event like a charity benefit. Her staff put me on the phone with her, so she could tell me how to relay her welcome and her support of the High Line to our guests. She had written her remarks herself. I was impressed by the effort she'd made to learn the details of the project while she was dealing with her legal case.

JOSH

I took Janice McGuire on a tour. She was a fellow community board member and the executive director of the Hudson Guild, a settlement house that provided social services in the neighborhood. She wanted to build bridges between newer, more affluent residents in Chelsea and the less advantaged residents who lived in the Fulton and Chelsea-Elliott houses, the two local subsidized housing complexes. And she had an empty office at Hudson Guild, which was located within the Chelsea-Elliott Houses, on West Twenty-sixth Street. She offered us the office at an absurdly low rent—something like $300 a month. We needed a bigger office, and moving there from the East Village would connect us with the community. We took it.

The offices hadn't been touched since the complex was built in the early 1950s. The walls were cinderblock, painted in a drab green. The heating and bathrooms barely functioned. But the Hudson Guild was an anchor in the community, with counseling and job-training services, a preschool, and a senior center. There was something great about coming to work and going down a hallway full of kids on their way to nursery school, or working at your desk and hearing them singing. The office was big enough to fit four desks. We could see a tiny sliver of the High Line from our window.

We posted an item on our e-mail newsletter asking for donated office furniture. A young pair of architects, Yen Ha and Ostap Rudakevych, replied, offering to help us design the space.

ROBERT

That fall, we hired Juliet Page from New Yorkers for Parks to fund-raise for us. Juliet loved the High Line and had helped us with our first foundation grants as a volunteer.

For the next four years, she ran all our fund-raising efforts. She was a one-woman band. She did our events, our year-end appeal, and she started our capital campaign. A lot of small

nonprofits don't like to spend money on development staff, but
you need to invest in fund-raising to grow.

JOSH

We had to pay Juliet a competitive salary. It was more than
Robert and I were making, which felt strange. She asked about
what benefits we offered; we didn't offer any at that point. She
also asked us to buy her an Aeron chair. She had one at New
Yorkers for Parks. We nickel-and-dimed her about the chair, and
she ultimately made a deal to buy the one she'd had at New
Yorkers for Parks. Because she was leaving a good job at an
established organization, we had to have a frank conversation
with her. We told her there were no guarantees at the High Line.
We hoped we would succeed, but she was taking a job with an
organization that might be gone tomorrow.

ROBERT

In late September, we presented the economic study to Dan
Doctoroff. We showed the feasibility of building a park on the
High Line, how much it would cost, and the value it would
generate for the City. Our estimated construction costs were
for a bare-bones version of a park on the High Line, using a
traditional greenway design vernacular—a simple paved walkway,
bordered by planters. We thought that in the end we were likely
to pursue a plan with greater design sophistication, with higher
costs, but for the purposes of this study, it was important to
keep cost estimates as low as possible. The presentation also
laid out a simple version of the transfer of development rights
mechanism that was ultimately used in the rezoning of West
Chelsea, which would allow owners of property under the High
Line to sell their unusable development rights above the
High Line to a number of other property owners in the
neighborhood.

JOSH

John said no one would read the study itself, which was
hundreds of pages long. What the study was good for was
making a nice *thunk* when you dropped it on the table, after you
gave your PowerPoint presentation. We had worked for weeks
on the PowerPoint.

Dan talked in that meeting about the mayor's larger plans for
the redevelopment of the West Side around the Olympics. This
would involve a major rezoning in Hell's Kitchen, the rezoning in
Chelsea, and a stadium on the rail yards.

He asked, "Do you think that the community likes the High
Line enough to make them supportive of the rezoning in West
Chelsea that includes it?"

Robert turned to me and said, "Josh is on the community
board—Josh, the community will like this, right?"

At that point I didn't know. The community board hadn't

taken a position on the High Line, and many of the members individually were fairly negative about it. But I knew the answer that everybody needed to hear was "yes," so that is the answer I gave.

It was also clear that Dan wanted our support of his larger vision in its entirety, including the stadium. That was fairly burdensome, because the stadium faced intense community opposition. Our project needed both the community and Dan to be happy, but this was not going to be easy.

Dan was going to meet with Chelsea Property Owners to give them a chance to present their study. We felt pretty good about our study. Dan seemed excited about the larger vision of the project, and how it might connect with his own big vision. It felt like we had a chance.

Ideas for the High Line

ROBERT

We started planning for a design competition. It wasn't going to be the kind of competition where the design that wins gets built. It couldn't be: we didn't have any rights, we didn't have any money, and the High Line was still in danger of being torn down. The competition would be just for ideas—and the ideas didn't have to be realistic, or fundable, or buildable.

The competition would free people up to think about the High Line in different ways. And it would get attention. Most people still didn't know what the High Line was, even people in the neighborhood. You'd mention the High Line and they'd go, "What?" Then you'd say, "You know, that elevated rail line," and they still wouldn't know. And then you'd say, "That dark thing with the pigeon droppings under it," and then they'd go, "Oh, yeah, that thing. I hate that thing."

JOSH

There are aspects of the High Line's progress that Robert had in his head from very early on and which he pursued with great determination. The design ideas competition was one of these.

He, more than I, latched on to a high level of design as being integral to the future of the High Line. I loved architecture. I loved beautiful design. But I didn't look at the project in as expansive terms as Robert did. I just loved the structure itself and wanted to save it.

ROBERT

John Alschuler urged us not to do the ideas competition. He said, "Look, people already think you're crazy. If you encourage people to submit ideas that are never going to happen, you're reinforcing the idea that this is just a dream." Gifford agreed. As

City Council speaker, he was trying to push the High Line as something that could actually happen.

JOSH

We got positive feedback from Dan's office throughout the fall, largely through Laurel Blatchford, whom we'd call from time to time; she told us that things were looking good. Finally, at the end of the year, Laurel said that the City was going to file with the Surface Transportation Board in Washington requesting a Certificate of Interim Trail Use to railbank the High Line. By doing that, they would effectively change City policy from one that favored demolishing the High Line to one that favored saving it.

It was our biggest victory yet. We now had the City as a partner. Not only had it dropped its opposition to the High Line, but it had done so in a way, with its STB filing, that indicated it was going to actively pursue transformation of the High Line into a trail or park.

You'd think champagne bottles would have been popping by the caseload, but that did not happen. Once again, I don't remember much about the good news, except for the work it generated. There was another press release to turn around, and this time the City had to sign off on it, too. Then, two days later, there was a piece in the *Times*, by David Dunlap: "On West Side, Rail Plan Is Up and Walking." We kept picking up the paper to read and reread it.

The change was so momentous that we found it hard to adjust to at first. Of all the powers that had been aligned against the High Line, the City had seemed the greatest. Now some casual observers even thought that saving the High Line was a done deal, which it definitely was not. The State, the railroad, and the Surface Transportation Board hadn't given their consent. And the Chelsea Property Owners still actively opposed it. There was so much that had to be done before we were assured of saving any part of the High Line. But for Robert and me, this victory changed the way that we looked at the High Line and what it meant to our lives. Now there was a chance that it might actually happen.

ROBERT

Now the Bloomberg administration fully supported the High Line, but if they'd only endorsed it and done nothing else, the project would have died. Everything about the High Line was complex, and it had to pass through so many different agencies and departments. City government is like the human body: the head, which is the Mayor's Office, may want to do something, but the body has a number of different parts that want to go their own way.

Laurel Blatchford was assigned to the High Line by Dan Doctoroff to make sure the project moved forward in a coordinated, efficient way. She helped us work on all fronts: legal, planning, economic development, and funding. Mayor Bloomberg's administration attracted a lot of people from the private sector who wanted to get things done. Dan Doctoroff, in particular, hired sharp people, like Laurel.

Dan told her the High Line was a priority, but she personally also shared our passion for the project. As at so many other times in the High Line's story, smart people were attracted to the High Line, people with the expertise to help us get the job done.

JOSH

Diane von Furstenberg had hosted an event for Save Gansevoort Market at her studio space on West Twelfth Street. We hoped that she might do something similar for the High Line. We asked Florent Morellet how to set it up, and he said, "Talk to Luisella." If you wanted to do anything with Diane, you went through Luisella Meloni. It was always fun to call her, because her melodic Italian accent made simple things feel exotic and rich.

We settled on a date in January. It was going to be a winter fund-raiser, but when the City changed its policy on the High Line, we turned it into a victory celebration. The invitation showed the line of the High Line as the stem of a martini glass.

Diane's studio was in a converted stable complex on West Twelfth Street, just south of the Meatpacking District. When you walked in, you saw a dramatic staircase that came down around a small bubbling pool. There were portraits of Diane by famous artists: Andy Warhol, Francesco Clemente. Past the stairs and the pool was a big, high-ceilinged space where Diane held her fashion shows and other events.

We've had a lot of fantastic events over the years, but this one was the first that felt like a real party, because of the City's new policy. From the ceiling, Bronson had hung a floating table shaped like the High Line and covered in crudités and hors d'oeuvres. It was more impressive than anything you imagined a group like ours putting together.

There is a photo from that night, of Robert and Diane and me—it captures the excitement of the moment. Diane is in the center, pulling back her hair in the glamorous way she has, and we're on either side of her, somehow separate and yet together.

ROBERT

We hired some new staff, all very young: Justin Rood as our office manager, and Olivia Stinson to help with the design ideas competition. We also hired Rick Little to get businesses to be on our "business map."

People assume that any preservation or community group is going to be anti-business, or anti-development, but we were pro-business. We recognized that the High Line was going to be good for businesses, and that those businesses could be our supporters. A lot of local businesses were start-ups like us. We wanted to make a map that showed the businesses and all the other things in the neighborhood that the High Line could connect.

Rick was an opera major from a liberal arts college and didn't have relevant expertise. He was also very shy. Why would we hire the shy guy with no expertise to go sell to businesses? But Rick proved to be, along with Juliet, one of those critical early employees who not only grew in the job but also helped to define our internal ethos. He soon became our de facto office manager, finance director, and human resources manager.

JOSH

The beginning of the Iraq War in March made me anxious. Justin read aloud off the computer in our Hudson Guild offices as the first bombs were falling. When Stephen and I went to the protests on the East Side, the police hemmed us all inside metal riot fences, like livestock. I'd been to many protests over the years—never had there been such restraints. I was worried that attacking Iraq would bring more anger back to United States—that George Bush had painted a fresh new target sign on New York City. I experienced a level of anxiety that sometimes made it hard for me to leave the house. My therapist gave me a prescription for these wonderful little pink pills, which helped.

ROBERT

That spring we focused on the ideas competition. I had decided that I didn't want to be spending all my time on the High Line if we weren't going to have an incredible design. We'd been to the Promenade Plantée, in Paris, but that design doesn't play off the unusualness of the structure: it is like that of a regular Parisian park, with rose trellises, an allée of trees, and a little water stream in the middle. I thought it would be a missed opportunity if we saved the High Line and then put a standard park up there.

To run the ideas competition, we hired Reed Kroloff. He was editor of *Architecture* magazine and also the boyfriend of Casey Jones, the architect who'd done the Design Trust study. Reed said, "You're not going to get big-name architects to compete, because you don't have much of a prize, and they're not going to waste their time on something that's never going to happen."

We did persuade some well-known architects to be on the jury—Stephen Holl, who did a famous early project about the High Line called "Bridge of Houses"; Bernard Tschumi, head of the architecture program at Columbia; Marilyn Jordan Taylor, who was heading Skidmore, Owings and Merrill; Julie Bargmann, who'd been working on the stadium plan and was encouraging the planners to keep the High Line; and Signe Nielsen, a landscape designer who'd worked on Hudson River Park. The other jurors were Murray Moss, from the design store Moss, in SoHo; Lynne Cooke, a curator at Dia Center for the Arts; Vishaan Chakrabarti, whom Amanda had hired to be director of the Manhattan office of the Department of City Planning; and Lee Compton, a community board member who lived near the High Line and was very supportive of our efforts.

JOSH

In April 2003, Community Board 4 finally voted on a resolution in favor of saving the High Line. It took almost four years for us to get the vote. When we did, in a meeting at St. Luke's–Roosevelt Hospital, it was 28 to 1. It was ultimately good that it took the board so long to get around to voting the issue. If the resolution had come up when we first started, they might have voted us down.

I was on the community board for about six years. My time there taught me how to work with large, difficult-to-manage groups that need to be carried along gently to reach one goal or another. I held a lot of one-on-one meetings with fellow board members to build goodwill for the High Line. I was lucky to get advice from other members who liked the High Line, such as Joe Restuccia, a developer of affordable housing in Hell's Kitchen, and Lee Compton, a Chelsea resident who went on to become Board 4's chair.

I slept well the night the community board voted in favor of the High Line. I still see the one woman who voted "no" in the neighborhood and at public meetings. We're friendly—sometimes we even agree on things—but she always speaks to me in a slightly sarcastic way, as if to say, I've got your number, you can't fool me.

ROBERT

The first entry to arrive for the ideas competition was drawn as a cartoon. It turned the High Line into a Mother Hubbard theme park, with the stairs built into a giant shoe. No other entries came in for a while after that. We were worried. We had done all this work for the competition, and we were going to end up with just this fairytale theme park.

In the end we received 720 entries from thirty-six countries. We had asked for the entries to be submitted on boards, because we didn't have the resources to mount them ourselves. With 720 of them, it was too much for our tiny office at Hudson Guild. We had to move them to an empty office space in the Starrett-Lehigh Building, which was lent to us by one of our supporters.

A few famous firms entered, including Polshek Partnership, the Hariri sisters, and 2x4, Michael Rock's graphic design firm. But most of the entries were from students and ordinary people. We had an entry that came from Iran—they had to ship it to Paris first and then have someone ship it from Paris to New York because you couldn't mail things here directly from Tehran after 9/11. An entry came from Russia that showed the High Line as a lizard, done in the style of an icon with gold paint. We had political manifestos—one submission had really strong black-and-white graphics and was called "Park Prison Pool." If you were going to imprison people, the proposal went, the public should have to see the prisoners, so they proposed building a prison within the I-beams of the High Line that you could look into while you were walking in the park; underneath, there would be a pool.

I had two favorites. An architecture student from Austria, Nathalie Rinne, proposed making the High Line into a mile-and-a-half-long swimming pool. The image of a lap pool running right through Manhattan was very beautiful. Another idea was from Front Studio, the firm of Yen Ha and Ostap Rudakevych, the two young architects who had designed our office space at Hudson Guild. They proposed leaving the landscape intact, as in the Joel Sternfeld photos, and putting a roller coaster on the Line. You'd be zooming up, looking into someone's apartment, zipping down, and doing flips over the city streets. These were not realistic ideas, but they made people think about the High Line in new ways.

The strongest common thread running through the entries was an appreciation for the existing landscape. People loved what was up there already.

Of the four finalists, none was realistic. One was called "Black Market Crawler." It talked about preserving the dark side of the High Line, and it pictured a woman shooting up in her leg. I was worried about what Gifford would think of that one.

We wanted to exhibit the entries in a high-profile location. I had fallen in love with Vanderbilt Hall in Grand Central Terminal. For a corporate event there, it cost almost $100,000 a day, but as a nonprofit we were able to cut a deal with them to have the exhibit for two weeks in the summer for $30,000.

It's complicated to do installations in Vanderbilt Hall. It sits over the Guastavino arches of the Oyster Bar, so you cannot have a heavy weight-load bearing down on any single point—you have to spread the weight out over a large footprint. Then there is the marble floor to worry about. And it's all under the MTA's jurisdiction, so there were many security issues. We would have only two days to install.

It's such a big room, and we worried that the competition boards would be dwarfed by it. A quarter million people walk through that space each day. What was going to make them stop for our competition? To help us figure out a solution, we met with LOT-EK, a small architecture firm with offices near the High Line. They were among the first architects to use shipping containers to create architectural forms; they had designed the Bohen Foundation, on West Thirteenth Street.

At LOT-EK, Ada Tolla and Giuseppe Lignano planned a large structure to house the exhibition. The front would be a movie theater-like video installation that faced onto the central path through Vanderbilt Hall. The scale of it, and the flickering images, would draw people in. On both sides would be huge vinyl panels that Paula Scher at Pentagram would design for us, blowing up Joel Sternfeld's images to billboard proportions. We would mount the finalists' competition boards under these and display more of the entries inside the structure, behind the video screen, several hundred in all.

The video was essential. It would capture people's attention and explain what the High Line was. A friend of mine, Jim Hitchcock, put me in touch with John Zieman, who produced and directed commercials and music videos. John made a great video for us. He interviewed key people and also got some great footage up on the High Line. The video really captured the spirit of what we were trying to do.

We decided to hold our summer benefit on the opening night of the exhibition: a cocktail party for a thousand people, followed by dinner for three hundred. It was so big because we invited everybody who entered the competition to come to the cocktail party for free. This was a huge undertaking for our small staff and for Josh and me. We got into our first really big fight about it.

JOSH

The ideas competition was something Robert had always wanted to do, and he drove it very hard, as he often does. It was a big lift for us, especially the exhibition at Grand Central. I was not convinced that we had to make design so central to our mission. I just wanted to save the High Line and open it to the public. Robert's perspective was, "It can't be a park like other parks. If it's like other parks, we've failed." That felt arrogant to me, more than I had signed on for.

The strain of producing the competition and the exhibition brought things to a head. There was the mad rush to get the competition papers together and launch the competition on the website. There was the physical demand of dealing with the entries that were arriving—each entry was 30 inches by 40 inches, and there were 720 of them. All the boards—there were mountains of them—had to be moved from our office to storage at Starrett-Lehigh, then to the jury site, then back to Starrett-Lehigh again, and then to Grand Central. Then there was the construction of the exhibition structure. At every stage of the process, everything was so last-minute. If you walked into Vanderbilt Hall twenty-four hours before the opening, you would have said there is no way this is going to happen.

We were both doing our other jobs, too, and we were exhausted. I often had to get up at four in the morning to write all the letters, press releases, and e-mail newsletters that were needed for the High Line. People would say, "Why are you e-mailing me at four in the morning?"

I'd been planning for a year to travel with Stephen in Sicily for my fortieth birthday and our twentieth anniversary, and the competition jury ended up being scheduled at the same time. I resented that Robert had scheduled it then, and Robert resented that I stuck to my travel plans and left him to do the jury alone.

When I came back from my trip, we met at Starrett-Lehigh to decide which boards would be included in the exhibition. The room had something wrong with it. There was dust in there, or maybe it was the glue from the boards, but if you spent more than half an hour there, you got a splitting headache and felt dizzy. Our fight started about individual boards, but it ended up being about everything.

ROBERT

We had to do our selections quickly, because I had an important meeting at Grand Central to get to. And there we were, fighting, with all these fumes and stacks of 720 competition boards.

I had to leave for my meeting, and I was still upset. Josh was considerate enough to offer me a sedative. I don't think I'd ever taken a sedative before. But I took the little pink pill, and it helped. I thought of it as a peace offering.

For better or for worse, the exhibition was an example of how we function as an organization. We often commit to more than seems prudent. Someone once told me that Friends of the High Line functions more like a political campaign than a nonprofit, mobilizing a lot of people to get behind something in very little time.

JOSH

We survived, and the exhibition did get finished in time. The star of opening night was Gifford Miller. He stood up on the podium in front of those one thousand people at the benefit cocktail party and announced that the City Council was making a $15.75 million allocation to the High Line, money that could be used to build the park, eventually. It was our greatest advance of the year, coming just six months after the new City policy.

Vanderbilt Hall is a terrific place to announce something good in, because of the acoustics—when people cheer, it sounds amazing.

That Council allocation created a sense of inevitability about the High Line, long before we won any of the approvals necessary to actually take it forward. We didn't have the Certificate of Interim Trail Use from the STB. The property owners were still challenging us in court. But we had $15.75 million for construction.

ROBERT

We had distributed comment cards to those assembled at the Grand Central exhibition. On my favorite one, the commenter wrote, "The High Line should be preserved, untouched, as a wilderness area. No doubt you will ruin it. So it goes." I tacked that above my desk. It spoke to my biggest fear: I loved what it was like up there, as it was. I was afraid that no matter what we designed, it would lose that magic. Until the day we opened, I was secretly scared that we were going to ruin it.

JOSH

Edward Norton, Robert Caro, Edie Falco, and Justin Theroux were at the benefit. I was excited that Kitty Carlisle Hart and Patty Hearst came, too. To me, Kitty and Patty represented two kinds of royalty. Kitty, at ninety-two, was a legend of the theater and of New York itself. How many times had I seen her face in the party pages, and now she was at our party, brought by Randy Bourscheidt, a friend of Robert's. And Patty's story had imprinted itself on me when I was a boy in Brookline, Massachusetts. I had been mesmerized by her phone calls from captivity, which played on the AM radio of our brown Plymouth Valiant. She was represented as an actress by the talent agency Stephen worked for, and Stephen had helped me invite her to the benefit.

At Grand Central, Kitty and Patty told us they wanted to see the High Line for themselves. Randy took us aside and told us that if we wanted Kitty to come, we would have to send a car for her. We still had very little money, so it seemed crazy to be hiring cars, but Kitty was Kitty, and so, a few days later, we sent a black car to bring her to the Thirty-fourth Street gate. She stepped out, perfectly coiffed, wearing a snug red dress and shiny black high heels. We helped her up the gravel embankment and onto the tracks. That was far enough for her. She looked all around, smiling into the sun, and said, "Isn't this marvelous! I hope you'll work fast, because I want to sing at your opening." And then the black car took her away.

Patty Hearst came with her daughter Gillian. Because of 9/11, security around the rail yards had been stepped up, and even though our tours were sanctioned by the railroad, sometimes three or four police officers would chase after us up there. We were about halfway around the rail yards section when the police came running at us from Thirty-fourth Street. Patty cried out, "I'm going to get arrested!" Her tone was like "Isn't this fun?" It was one of my favorite High Line tours. Gillian has been a supporter ever since; she works on the committee of every benefit we do.

The matter of the High Line had been before the Surface Transportation Board for some fifteen years at this point. The STB is a federal regulatory board—it oversees all rail systems in the United States—but you don't read about it a lot in the papers. Now, all of a sudden, it was regularly landing in the *Times* with the High Line story. We had Congressman Nadler pushing for us, along with the two senators, Schumer and Clinton.

The STB held a hearing in New York City. We testified in coordination with the City. A year before, we'd been pitching to Dan Doctoroff. Now we were working alongside him. After the hearing, we gave a tour of the High Line to the head of the STB, Roger Nober. He seemed impressed.

When the computers shut down, the lights went out, and the air-conditioner stopped, we laughed. We were used to the systems failing at the Hudson Guild office. When we sensed it was something bigger, the first thing that came to mind is, the city has been hit, it's another 9/11. When it turned out to be a blackout, it gave everything a festive mood, even as we learned that much of the Northeast had been left without electricity. We could forget about the High Line and go home in the middle of a summer afternoon. I cooked spaghetti on my gas stove by candlelight for Stephen, his dad, and our friend Joyce. The old trees and town houses of West Twenty-first Street were beautiful in the darkness. On Eighth Avenue, in front of Rawhide, hundreds of men had gathered in the night. Shirtless, in their little shorts, they could not be contained by the sidewalk and had filled the street, pressed up against each other—it was an orgy on Eighth Avenue.

Josh and I really weren't getting along after that big fight. He was thinking about leaving.

My friend Edmund Bingham is a coach for executives, and I asked him if he could help. He met with us individually and then met with us together. There was one meeting at Josh's apartment where we were really yelling at each other. I said some mean, hurtful things.

I was open to conflict at work, but that was not Josh's style. This kind of conflict was deeply, deeply upsetting to him.

I'm always looking to start a new project, then to do a new project on top of the new project. I kept pushing the organization to do more, whereas Josh felt, why do we need to take on more and more, why do we put such stress on the organization and ourselves?

After that meeting with Edmund, Josh changed the way he dealt with me. He recognized that I was pushier, and he started letting me have my way unless it was something he felt was very important. He would save issues and raise them only when absolutely necessary.

We're not close friends. I have never been to dinner at Josh's house. We've had plenty of meals together, but all of them are at work or in restaurants and about work. We talk about personal things and we care about each other, but we have a professional relationship. Some people assume that we're lovers or that we dated once, but one of the keys to our success is that we've been able to separate our roles and our relationship. It's my longest-term relationship. I've had boyfriends for three years, or five years, but this relationship has lasted twelve years. I view it as an important accomplishment that we've been able to keep working together and have built this organization.

Normally just one person runs an organization. You can pretend it's not true, but an organization's success is often dependent on whether people like the person in charge. If someone doesn't like the person running the place, or if they have a conflict with the leader, they won't support it. Whereas, if you have two people running the place, you can dislike one of them, but there's still the other one to like.

Florent told me it was the same for him and Jo. One of them would piss someone off, but that person would still support Save Gansevoort Market because the other one was there. The organization wasn't driven by a single personality.

JOSH

Jo and Florent got their final win before we did. In the fall of 2003, the Landmarks Commission announced it was going to designate a big chunk of the Meatpacking District as a historic district. Save Gansevoort Market had saved Gansevoort Market.

The lines for the historic district had been drawn when the City still wanted to tear the High Line down, and so the proposed district didn't include the High Line or the buildings adjacent to it. This was a loss, because the powers of protection from the historic designation would not be in place around the High Line. But it was still a big victory. It showed that the tide was turning for unusual projects like ours.

City Planning

ROBERT

That fall, the public planning process for the West Chelsea
rezoning began, with a forum held by City Planning in the
Hudson Guild meeting room at Fulton Houses, on
Ninth Avenue.

The Bloomberg administration, under Dan and Amanda's
leadership, wanted to create a newly rezoned West Chelsea
District, between Sixteenth and Thirtieth streets, with the
High Line at its center. Its key would be the transfer of
development rights.

Amanda and her team, led by Vishaan Chakrabarti, did the
work of putting together the rights transfer system for the
district around the High Line, inspired by what had been done
before around Grand Central Terminal and the Theater District.
The framework would allow the unused development rights
above the High Line to be sold to receiving sites up and down
Tenth and Eleventh avenues. Our main opponents, the Chelsea
Property Owners, including Edison Parking and many others,
owned most of these unused development rights. The hope was
that if we could find another way for them to monetize their
unused rights, their opposition to the High Line would go away.

Amanda also felt strongly that the growing art gallery district
was one of the most interesting things about the neighborhood.
The galleries had been priced out of SoHo and had moved to
Chelsea. If the rezoning created too much opportunity for
residential development, the resulting economic pressure on
property owners to develop housing could force the galleries
out of West Chelsea, too. Nobody wanted the galleries to be
pushed out by housing, after they'd been pushed out of SoHo
by high-end retail. To manage this, Amanda and Vishaan wanted
to keep a manufacturing designation for the middle of the
blocks, which would prevent residential development in the
areas where most of the galleries were located.

Amanda and Vishaan also proposed controls to shape new
construction next to the High Line, so that there would be sun,
air, and views on the High Line, and opportunities to build stairs
and elevators to the High Line within the shells of new buildings.
The controls would forbid building over the High Line, to keep
the park open to the sky and to preserve sight lines. Previously,
you could build over it if you left enough space for trains to
pass through. Now this would be prohibited. These restrictions
wouldn't apply to the area south of Sixteenth Street, in the
Meatpacking District, where the community had fought against
a rezoning. The old, less restrictive manufacturing designation
would remain there, which ultimately allowed the Standard
Hotel to be built over the High Line. And at the other end,

around the rail yards, the City was pursuing the Olympics and the stadium plan, so that area was outside the proposed West Chelsea district, too.

JOSH

The High Line was only one of the forces shaping the zoning. You had a group fighting to keeping new buildings as low as possible, and a group pushing for more affordable housing. There was also a smaller group pushing for the retention of manufacturing space, not just for the galleries, but also to support a continued manufacturing sector.

Then there were the property owners under the High Line and all around the neighborhood. Most of them originally wanted the High Line torn down, but now they began advocating for as much leeway as possible to develop large, profitable buildings. Jerry Gottesman from Edison Properties told us he wasn't actually as opposed to the High Line itself as he was to the neighborhood's manufacturing-focused zoning designation, called M1-5. Jerry said that M1-5 was a "useless, anti-progress" designation, one that left him with no opportunity to profitably develop his properties, although it was the same zoning designation that had allowed him to buy his properties cheaply in the first place. Joe Rose, meanwhile, was also planning a development in the neighborhood, if it were to be rezoned. Joe told us that had we come to him earlier in the Giuliani administration, before the decision to tear down the High Line had been made, he might have taken a different position. "The High Line had been an impediment for so many years," he said. "You and your group changed it into a catalyst, but back then it was still just an impediment."

We started meeting with people in the keep-buildings-low group and in the affordable housing group. The reality was moving the development rights away from High Line sites was going to mean that some buildings were going to be taller. And in order for the economics of the development rights transfers to work, there had to be a major chunk of market-rate housing in the formula, which was not what the affordable housing group wanted to hear. Yet we built relationships with these groups, and found a way to voice support for their position when we spoke, even if their priorities differed from ours. We didn't want to set up a dynamic in which the High Line was perceived as being in competition with these other good interests.

ROBERT

Often when the City or a developer puts out a rezoning plan, they propose big buildings, which they can then negotiate down with various constituencies. But Vishaan's strategy was to put a plan out there that he thought made sense at the start. People weren't happy with that. The developers wanted greater density and taller buildings. The community wanted shorter buildings. There wasn't much room to negotiate.

JOSH

Now that there was a real chance the High Line could happen, assembling the funds for it became important. As part of the Design Trust study, we'd looked at pots of federal money that the High Line might be eligible to receive. The most promising source of federal funds was in the multiyear transportation bills, but they came up for a vote only once every five years. These were highway bills, but there were smaller programs within them that funded walkways and bike trails and parks. As each bill moved forward, lawmakers could add "priority projects" or "demonstration projects"—earmarks, really. The expiration of the most recent bill, TEA-21, was approaching. It would soon be time for lawmakers to reauthorize it. This was an opportunity for us to apply for major federal funding.

Jim Capalino recommended that we hire representation in Washington, so Robert and I took the train down and interviewed lobbyists. We ended up hiring Jack Schenendorf, from Covington and Burling, which still represented us, pro bono, for our filings at the Surface Transportation Board. Jack didn't put on a show. All by himself, in his quiet, soothing voice, he walked us through the steps we'd need to take. By the time he'd made it through the third or fourth step, he'd lost me in the land of sessions and conferences and markups. But I had full confidence he could lead us through this—and Robert did, too.

Jack had strong relationships with the committee's Republican leadership. Our group was comprised mostly of Democrats. In the Bush years, we knew it would help us to have a lobbyist who worked well with Republicans.

ROBERT

Following the ideas competition, we held a community input session, to reassure the community that we weren't just going to pick one of these crazy designs, and also to hear them, so their priorities could inform the design.

Alan Boss, who ran the old flea market on Sixth Avenue, also owned Metropolitan Pavilion, an events facility on Eighteenth Street, and he lent us a large space to use for our meeting. About four hundred people came, and we divided them into tables of ten. Each table had a facilitator, either a High Line staff member or one of our better volunteers. We projected some of the entries from the ideas competition, and a larger selection was leaning on the walls around the edges of the room. John Alschuler led the discussion, talking about the big picture of the High Line in the neighborhood. Then the groups talked among themselves about what they liked and didn't like about the entries. Each table elected one person to present their ideas, and those presenters spoke, one by one, to the larger group. We recorded it all on video and compiled the notes into a summary that was distributed later. We would end up doing many more sessions like this. It was an effective way for everyone to be involved.

JOSH

Scott Lauer, an architect who had volunteered for the High Line, started a nonprofit called Open House New York. It was inspired by an organization in London that, on a certain day of the year, opened up sites that were usually closed to the public. He was assembling a list of sites in New York that were usually closed, and asked if we could include the High Line.

We wanted to do it, but there was no way the railroad was going to let us. The liability issues were too great. We said, "What if we find a great space that looks out onto the High Line?" We talked to the owner of an old warehouse building next to the High Line at 511 West Twenty-fifth Street. To our surprise, he let us use the roof. There was a massive old water tower, and the space underneath it was very dramatic, and if you leaned over the parapet, you had a High Line view.

When I arrived at the site that morning, there was already a line by the door. By the end of the day, the roof was packed with people leaning over the edge. Those who couldn't fit onto the roof had gone to the floors below and opened windows and were hanging out from hallways and galleries. The entire building was literally overflowing with people. It made us realize how many people wanted to be part of the High Line. We'd been so busy that we hadn't noticed the interest growing.

ROBERT

At cocktail parties, people started asking us, "Aren't you fighting the stadium at the rail yards?" Dan had brought in the Jets, who would pay for the stadium and play their games there. When it wasn't being used for football, it would function as a convention hall, and with alterations it could also be used for the 2012 Olympics.

Alex Garvin, the director of planning for New York's 2012 Olympic bid, had shown us the original plans for the stadium, and they did not include the High Line. Then the Jets ownership hired Kohn Pedersen Fox, and they hired Julie Bargmann, a landscape architect, to consult.

The story we heard was that KPF was creating a shtick—they needed some kind of positive identity for this stadium—and they were looking at the old piers, with their gantries and outrigging, for inspiration. Julie told them, "You have a shtick that is here already: the High Line running around the site. Why invent something when you have the real thing right here?" She had an ally in Jay Cross, the president of the Jets, who had walked on the High Line at the rail yards and was interested in the idea of incorporating it into the stadium plan. Parts of the structure would have to be removed and rebuilt, but the easement that was crucial for railbanking could be maintained. This had made it possible for Dan to push for both projects, the High Line and the stadium.

JOSH

Dan made it clear that he expected our support for the stadium, while our supporters in the community made it clear that they detested the stadium. It had become a lightning rod for the most fervent community opposition you could imagine.

We depended on the support of both Dan and the community. We couldn't go forward without both of them. So we began walking a fine line, saying, "We're Friends of the High Line. Our issue is the High Line. We don't take positions on things besides the High Line."

ROBERT

The debate had gone far beyond the boundaries of the neighborhood. Business leaders supported the Olympics bid as a post-9/11 economic revitalization program and a source of civic pride. The whole City was talking about it.

I told Dan that we could make positive public comments about the fact that the stadium and the High Line could exist together, and we could express gratitude to the Jets for making that aspect of the plan possible, but we couldn't actively support the stadium without completely undermining our community support. He wasn't happy about it, but he kept his team working hard to advance the High Line even though we weren't actively supporting him on something he cared about deeply. It was the same with the community. They were angry with us that we weren't more vocally opposed, but they did not take out that anger on the High Line itself.

I went to a stadium hearing at the City Council. It was filled with union people and businesspeople who supported the stadium, and just as many community people who were against it. You had to sign up to speak by filling out a card and checking a box labeled "for" or "against." I wrote my name and then drew another box that said "neither" and checked that. The clerk said, "You can't do that. You have to say 'for' or 'against.'" I said, "I'm neither for nor against. I'm neutral." He said, "Oh, both sides must hate you, then."

JOSH

Our office at Hudson Guild was cheap but way too small for our growing staff—there were six of us now, and Robert and I had gone back to working at home because there wasn't enough room. Hudson Guild, meanwhile, was planning a major renovation, emptying the building, and so, during the last week of 2003, we moved to a space in the Meatpacking District, in a loft building at Fourteenth and Washington streets.

It was twelve blocks south, and an entirely different world. Stylish women in fur-trimmed coats rode up in the elevator with you, headed to Edris, a hair salon with minimalist flower arrangements near the door. You'd catch a glimpse of the handsome hipster hairdressers as you went by. The smell of shampoo and perms followed you down the creaky floorboards to our office, which faced west over a row of meatpacking plants. You could turn your head and look out the window at the meat being loaded and unloaded by men in bloodied white coats under the corrugated steel awnings. Every once in a while we'd all let out a collective groan when a Dumpster of meat scraps was upturned into a waiting dump truck. Seagulls rested on top of the awnings, swooping down to snatch scraps from the cobblestones.

From the roof, there were great views of the southern end of the High Line, running down to Gansevoort Street. Light off the river filled the office on winter afternoons, turning everything orange as the evening progressed.

ROBERT

In early 2004 our winning verdict in the Article 78 lawsuit against the City was overturned. The City had appealed, not wanting to allow a precedent to stand that would require them to take similar cases through the land use review process in the future. We appealed the new verdict and took it to the State Supreme Court. We lost that appeal, but it didn't matter now, because Mayor Bloomberg had changed City policy to support the High Line, and we were working closely with City Hall to carry the project forward.

JOSH

In February, one of the first major public hearings on the stadium plan for the rail yards took place in a theater on Forty-second Street. The union supporters arrived early, followed by community residents. It was so crowded that we nearly didn't make it in the door.

The challenge presented to us by the stadium wasn't only a political one. We were going to lose a big chunk of the High Line if the stadium got built. Even though the site occupied three entire city blocks, between Thirtieth and Thirty-third streets, and Eleventh Avenue and the West Side Highway, it wasn't really big enough for a stadium. The High Line wrapped around the site on three sides, occupying precious ground. To fit in the stadium, they would have to remove parts of the High Line, which was obviously something we did not like. But we worked with Dan Doctoroff and the Bloomberg administration to show how the future rail viability of the High Line's easement could be maintained, even if you removed the entire structure on the western yards. We weren't planning to run trains on the High Line again, but preserving the easement was critical to our plan to use the federal railbanking program to reuse the High Line as a park.

ROBERT

Ever since the Surface Transportation Board hearings the previous summer, when we testified alongside Dan Doctoroff, we'd been working in coordination with the City, in our own separate channels, toward the same goals. First, the City would rezone the neighborhood, which would provide a new way for the property owners under the High Line to harness the value of their development rights. With the rezoning in place, the property owners would stop litigating. Without the litigation, the Surface Transportation Board would issue a Certificate of Interim Trail use, and CSX would donate the High Line to the City, allowing it to be railbanked. The structure would become City property, managed by the Parks Department. Only then would the City be able spend any funds on designing and building a public park on it—it could not spend money building something it wasn't going to own.

JOSH

We worked with Congressman Nadler to secure federal appropriations funding that could be used to pay for a design contract in advance of City ownership, so when the High Line changed hands, the design would already be done and the City could start building immediately. The clock was ticking—we had the rare good fortune of having the support of both the mayor and the City Council. We expected this unified support to last just a few years, and we wanted to get as much done as we could while we had it.

ROBERT

John Alschuler sat us down in his office and said, "We're always talking about how to build the High Line, but we also have to deal with the operations side, too. Let's have a frank talk about where that money is going to come from." He said, "It really depends on how you see the future of your organization. Your name is Friends of the High Line. Do you see yourselves as a 'friends' group?"

Typically, in parks work, friends groups are off to the side. Somebody else, usually the government, pays for the park and runs it, and the friends group raises a bit more for special programs, or plants some extra trees. So John's question was, "Do you see yourself in that side role, or do you see yourself as the entity that's controlling the park and guiding its future?"

Betsy Barlow Rogers and the Central Park Conservancy had always been models for us. Theirs was an existing park, but a group of private citizens had come along, saved it from ruin, and then gone on to manage and operate it, raising the majority of funds to do so. Bryant Park was another great example of a group of private citizens taking one of the most dangerous, worst-maintained parks in New York and turning it into a jewel.

The City didn't have enough money to maintain the parks it already had. This new park on the High Line was not going to be an ordinary park with ordinary needs. It was thirty feet in the air. It ran through buildings. It was going to need a group like ours to fund-raise for it. At the same time, we were also hearing from donors such as Donald Pels, who told us, "If I'm going to continue to give money, I'm going to want to give it to the organization that's running the High Line, not some other organization that doesn't have the will or the power to keep your vision alive."

JOSH

Neither Robert nor I ever felt that we would stand off to the side. But ultimately to occupy the central role, like that of the Central Park Conservancy, would mean stepping up and being the park's primary funder—forever, basically. This was no longer an effort to fight demolition of the High Line. We were setting up an organization that was aiming to run a public park in New York City.

ROBERT

The Bloomberg administration was always open to this idea of a public-private partnership, but once they began actively carrying the High Line forward, they could have easily elbowed us aside. But the administration respected what we'd learned in the years before they came into office, and they let us work closely with them to select a design team, even though it would be a City-owned property, built with a large amount of City money.

We'd done the ideas competition, but that was not for a specific design. We still didn't know exactly what we wanted to see on the High Line. What we did know was that we wanted it to be open to the public and we wanted the experience to be as special and as unique as the High Line itself and as the landscape that already existed up there.

Laurel Blatchford at City Hall took the lead in setting up a steering committee to select a design team. There were five members from the mayor's side of City Hall: Dan Doctoroff; Amanda Burden; Patricia E. Harris, the first deputy mayor; Andrew Alper, the head of the Economic Development Corporation; and Adrian Benepe, the parks commissioner. Friends of the High Line got four seats, which we filled with me, Josh, Phil, and Gary. Gifford Miller, as speaker of the City Council, got one seat. Elected officials often assign their seats on boards or committees to representatives, because they don't have time to go to all the meetings. Gifford assigned his seat to one of our new board members, Barbaralee Diamonstein-Spielvogel. This made it more of a five-to-five dynamic, but we knew that we would have to defer to the City in the end.

JOSH

The commissioners usually had staff members sit in for them in working meetings. Erik Botsford represented Amanda Burden, Jennifer Hoppa and Joshua Laird represented Adrian Benepe and Parks, and Len Greco represented EDC. Laurel (who'd gone to work at HPD, Housing Preservation and Development) had been replaced by Marc Ricks. It seemed that Marc was carrying other important projects for Dan Doctoroff, along with the High Line. He spent a lot of those meetings tapping at his BlackBerry.

ROBERT

Up to that point, Josh and I had done everything related to design, with the guidance of our board, including Gary Handel, who is an architect. But these new meetings with the City ran for hours, and some of the issues that came up could be addressed only by someone with a design background. We decided we needed an architect on our staff full time, to oversee Friends of the High Line's role in the design team selection and ultimately to work with the design team we selected. The City would hold the contract to build the park on the High Line, but if it ended up running the park, we wanted to be involved in every aspect of its design and construction.

Peter Mullan, an architect at Polshek Partnership, had been one of our volunteers. He and I had gone to Princeton together but didn't really know each other. Olivia Douglas, one of our first board members, knew him better. One evening, while at Olivia's birthday party at a bar on Fifteenth Street called Passersby, I started talking to Peter about the High Line.

JOSH

There were times when it felt like a burden for Robert and me to be carrying everything. What if we got tired and quit, or got hit by a bus? It felt as if the High Line would grind to a halt. When Peter came in, it was the first time I felt that if something happened to Robert and me, someone else would carry things forward. Peter had the same kind of energy and passion for the High Line that we had.

Four Teams, Four Visions

ROBERT

First we issued an RFQ, a "request for qualifications," asking firms to join together in teams of architects, landscape architects, planners, designers, and engineers.

One of the questions we had was "Should the team's lead be an architect or a landscape architect?" We decided the team could put whomever they wanted in the leadership position. If I could do it over again, I'd require a landscape architect to be in the lead.

JOSH

Robert viewed the High Line as a landscape primarily, and I was always more interested in it as a structure. Maybe this was because of the way I had first become interested in the High Line, staring up at its steel columns and girders from the street. Also, I'd read Jane Jacobs right before we started. I wanted the High Line to have the human vitality she describes on the city's best streets. The plants were less interesting to me.

ROBERT

We received fifty-one entries and narrowed those down to seven, and then we did interviews with those seven designers, to learn how they would approach the High Line.

One team said, "The first thing you should do is just bulldoze what's on top of the High Line, put in fresh dirt, and then think about what to do next."

JOSH

It was the most radical thing you could have said. People's jaws dropped, because a kind of cult had developed around the existing landscape. But we ended up doing exactly what that team said we would have to do. Deep down, I think we all knew we'd have to do it—we were in a state of collective denial.

There was also a young team that Friends of the High Line pushed for, called OpenMeshWork (a combination of three small firms where various members worked). This team probably wasn't ready for a big project like the High Line, but then, we hadn't been ready for it, either, when we started out. Plus, we wanted at least one real underdog in the mix. OpenMeshWork had great ideas. One of our favorites was for a ceremony modeled after the Running of the Bulls in Pamplona, only here it would be "The Running of the Jets." Everyone in Chelsea would run up the High Line, chased by the Jets in uniform, trying not to be tackled, and then they'd all pour into the stadium, to thunderous applause.

We had big hopes for a team headed by Peter Latz, who had designed a famous park in a factory complex at Duisburg-Nord, in Germany. Instead of tearing down the old gas tanks, Latz's design reused them as park elements. Latz said that the challenge in New York was the High Line's narrowness, that there was very little space for both walkways and plantings. The solution he proposed was to build a trellis that would arch over the entire High Line. Everything would be paved except for the beds at the edges, where you'd plant vines to grow up over the trellis, creating a kind of green tunnel.

Amanda said, "That's interesting, but we like the views you get from the High Line, the perspectives it gives you on the city, and this proposal shuts you off."

ROBERT

We had planned to narrow the seven teams down to three, but when we did the voting at City Hall, we came up with four. They were Zaha Hadid with Balmori Associates; James Corner Field Operations, Diller Scofidio + Renfro, and Piet Oudolf; Steven Holl Architects with Hargreaves Associates; and Michael Van Valkenburgh with D.I.R.T. Studios and Beyer Blinder Belle.

We gave all four teams $25,000 each, which ended up covering only a fraction of their costs. Midway through the process, we scheduled interviews and went to each team's offices.

My money was on Michael Van Valkenburgh. He had a fantastic team: ARO, architects who had worked with Rem Koolhaas on the SoHo Prada store; Michael Rock with 2x4, a graphics firm that had submitted an entry for our ideas competition; and Julie Bargmann, the landscape architect who'd lobbied for the High Line with the Jets. Van Valkenburgh was already working on the Chelsea section of Hudson River Park, Brooklyn Bridge Park, and Teardrop Park at Battery Park City, and so there were people on the committee who felt that Michael's mark might be on too many other city parks already.

JOSH

The Van Valkenburgh team showed a real affection for the self-seeded landscape. They treated the wilderness on the High Line like a big green animal, a rare creature that lived up there, nesting in the gravel, and that had to be kept alive no matter what.

ROBERT

Steven Holl partnered with the landscape architect George Hargreaves. Steven's office overlooked the High Line, and it was intriguing to have one of the best architects in the world, who had been thinking about the High Line every day, for many years, competing to design the project.

JOSH

Steven's "Bridge of Houses" proposal in 1981 was the reason that every architecture professor and student knew about the High

Line. At the start of his presentations, he showed an old black-and-white photo of himself sitting in a chair amidst the rubble of the High Line, long before any of us had ever set foot up there.

ROBERT

Zaha Hadid had just won the Pritzker Architecture Prize. A few months earlier, when Herbert Muschamp, the architecture critic for the *Times*, had joined me on a tour, the first thing he said when we stepped out onto the High Line was "Zaha." He said her work had a linear quality that would be just right for the High Line. Herbert smoked all through that tour. Laurie Izes, from the railroad, kept telling him it was prohibited to smoke up there. He would drop the cigarette, and then a minute later he would light up a new one.

Zaha's team set about creating something completely new. She partnered with landscape architect Diana Balmori and the head of Skidmore, Owings and Merrill, Marilyn Jordan Taylor, who had been one of our ideas competition jurors. It was an interesting combination, SOM and Zaha Hadid, the practical with the wild.

In Zaha's approach, there were very few plants and no trees. It was this swooping white landscape that looked like it had been molded out of plastic. I asked her, "Do you not like trees?" She said, "Trees are things that architects put in the plan when they don't know what to do with a space." I liked that she wasn't trying to bullshit us. But it also made me realize she's wasn't the right fit.

JOSH

The Field Ops/DS+R team won many of us over at their first presentation. They described the High Line as a ruin, a found object. Liz Diller used the word *illicit*: you had crawl under a fence, and you entered a forbidden, secret area that had an aura of past sex and drugs. This team loved the High Line's dark and mysterious quality, which I was also drawn to.

ROBERT

Field Operations and Diller Scofidio + Renfro weren't sure of their approach, and they argued with each other about it at the presentation. How do you find the balance between preserving the magic that is up there and creating something new? I'd recently read *The Leopard* and had come across the famous quote, "If you want things to stay as they are, things will have to change." It summed up my developing thoughts about the design.

I liked the members of this team, but one of our board members had told me, "Don't pick a design team based on personality. Pick it on their work." When I told Phil Aarons this, he said, "Don't believe it. We're going to be working with these people. Pick people you want to work with."

JOSH

The plan was to end the competition with an exhibition called "Four Teams, Four Visions," held at the Center for Architecture, which had just opened its new space on LaGuardia Place.

I was thrilled when Ariel Kaminer, an editor from the *Times* Arts and Leisure section, returned my call. She would assign Julie Iovine to cover the exhibition if we gave them an exclusive "curtain raiser"—a glimpse of the designs before they were shown. None of the teams had been prepared to deliver early work for the press, but they all hustled to complete a few images. The Sunday before the exhibition, the images from the four teams filled a full page in the *Times*.

On the day of the deadline, we got two sets of boards from each firm. One set went to the Center for Architecture. The duplicate set went to Diane von Furstenberg's studio on West Twelfth Street, where we were previewing the exhibition at our summer benefit—Diane's cocktail party, which was followed by dinner at the Phillips de Pury auction house.

Florent dropped by Diane's cocktail party dressed as Marie Antoinette, as he always did on July 14, because he hosted an annual Bastille Day party at his restaurant. That year, his Marie Antoinette was High Line inspired, with a train running around her wig and another train running around her bustle.

Things went downhill when we moved on to dinner at Phillips de Pury. The air-conditioning didn't work, and we were all drenched with sweat. The cater-waiter staff had been selected for their looks rather than for their skills, and dinner still had not landed on the tables by 10:30. Barbaralee Diamonstein-Spielvogel, presiding over a table of twenty hungry, thirsty friends, tried to charm her waiter into bringing water and bread by telling him he had a delightful southern accent. He said, "That is not an accent, ma'am. I'm just drunk."

ROBERT

Kurt Andersen, who at that time wrote a regular column in *New York* magazine called "The Imperial City," moderated a panel discussion with all four design teams at the Center for Architecture. Each of the designers talked for so long that we had time for only one question. The place was packed, far beyond capacity. The press covered the overflowing crowds as much as the panel itself.

JOSH

Picking a winner wasn't easy. Anytime you eliminated a team, you were eliminating a possible future for the High Line.

In the end, the front runners were the Steven Holl team and the Field Ops/DS+R team. There was a part of me that longed for it to be Steven Holl, because of his history with the High Line, because I loved his work, and because he hadn't built anything major in New York City—it would be poetic justice for the High Line to be his first major New York commission.

His team's proposal included built forms that would be added to the High Line, and dramatic removals—cuts that would allow light to shine through to the street, waterfalls to cascade through the girders, and stairs to be woven through larger cuts. They would treat the High Line as if it were a suspended green valley in Manhattan's Alps, which I found to be an apt way of looking at how this floating ribbon of grasses ran through the towering warehouses and factories that surrounded it.

ROBERT

Field Ops/DS+R put a new walkway system at the core of their approach. It featured concrete planks that would comb into the landscaping. The walkways could be put together from a kit of parts—planks in different shapes and sizes that could be used in different ways. The plants would push up between the planks, just as they did between the gravel ballast of the tracks, blurring the line between the hard walkways and the soft plantings. It would almost be like nature trying to claw back the manmade structure and reclaim it.

They proposed cutting into the structure to bring the stairs through the steel girders—a strategy we'd seen in other proposals. They also showed something they called a "flyover," where the path ramped up from the surface of the High Line and flew through a canopy of trees. We liked that idea but didn't think we would actually build it.

Ric Scofidio said, "My job as an architect is to save the High Line from architecture." Thousands of architects have looked at the High Line as an exercise for building things. His team, however, focused on stripping things away and exposing the structure instead of adding to it.

The team also had a compelling vision for the plants. The Dutch plantsman Piet Oudolf was on this team, and the photos of his past work made you think of an idealized version of the natural landscape that we'd come to love on the High Line. Piet composed grasses and perennials in naturalistic ways, and he left the dead material on the plants in winter, to create sculptural shapes in the snow. When you looked at these photos, you thought, If there is anyone who can create something as beautiful as the High Line in its natural state, it is Piet.

JOSH

The committee was leaning toward the Field Ops/DS+R team, but we were nervous. We kept hearing from architects and landscape experts that the team's plan was creative, original, and beautiful, but that it would be unbuildable and impossible to maintain.

ROBERT

Traditionally in a competition, when it comes down to the
finalists, you go visit projects they've built. James and Ric and Liz
might disagree when I say this, but at the time, this team hadn't
built much. There was no project we could go visit. James
Corner Field Operations had designed the Fresh Kills Park at the
landfill on Staten Island, but it had not been built yet. Diller
Scofidio + Renfro's biggest completed project was called the
Blur Building, a temporary structure in the middle of a lake in
Switzerland. It was built of pipes that emitted steam, meant to
evoke a cloud, and it had been up for only two months, and
then came down. In New York, their design for the Brasserie, a
restaurant in the Seagram Building, had the reputation of being
one of the most expensive restaurant interiors ever built, which
wasn't exactly a ringing endorsement. They were working on the
Institute of Contemporary Art in Boston, and they'd been
selected to do the renovations at Lincoln Center, but neither of
those projects was finished. They were most famous in New
York for their retrospective at the Whitney. Many people
thought of them more as conceptual art architects than
real-building architects.

I went to get advice from Vishaan Chakrabarti. He said, "Do
you want something that you know will be good, or do you
want to take a risk for something great?"

When he put it like that, it was an easy question to answer.

JOSH

There was debate around the table at City Hall, but no actual
conflict. At one point Nanette Smith, who represented Deputy
Mayor Patti Harris, said, "As we're deciding, I think we should
listen carefully to what Friends of the High Line is saying,
because they've been doing this for a lot longer than we have."
It was an incredible thing for her to have said, given that the
power was all on their side of the table.

ROBERT

It says a lot about the Bloomberg administration, that they were
willing to take a risk and pick a team that would bring such an
innovative and untested design to a public space in New
York City.

JOSH

We selected the Field Ops/DS+R team in late summer,
with the expectation of announcing the selection after
Labor Day.

In drumming up press for the exhibition, we'd reached out to
Nicolai Ouroussoff, an architecture critic from Los Angeles who
was coming to the *Times* to replace Herbert Muschamp. We
took Nicolai on the High Line and arranged for him to talk with
all four teams.

Shortly after the vote at City Hall, Nicolai called and said he knew which team we'd selected and that he was running a review in advance of our announcement—he'd scooped us. After the vote, we'd confidentially given the news to all the teams. We never figured out who told Nicolai.

It would be his first review as the critic for the *Times*. Each morning at the corner bodega, I would take a deep breath before flipping to the Arts section. On the morning of August 12, there it was across the section's front page: "An Appraisal: Gardens in the Air Where the Rail Once Ran." Nicolai had seen all the same things we'd seen in the team's approach, its blend of old and new, its appreciation for the grittiness of the High Line, the ingenuity of the walkway system. As I read it, I felt that he had just catapulted us, and that we were soaring.

ROBERT

We'd planned to do a press conference to announce the design team, but after Nicolai's article, there wasn't a lot of news there. There'd been other very important advances, though. While we'd been wrapped up in selecting a design team, Dan Doctoroff and Marc Ricks had secured the State's consent to join the federal application for railbanking; with the State on board, CSX also agreed to join. Only the underlying property owners were still opposing. At the same time, the mayor had decided to make a $27.5 million funding allocation to the High Line, which, when added to the City Council's $15.75 million, gave us $43.25 million for construction. We had Dan to thank for this new funding. Once he committed to the idea of the High Line, his embracing of our vision and his determination to get it built were among our greatest assets. He had made the High Line a priority project for the administration, and even when we didn't give him the support he wanted for the stadium, he continued to give his full support to the High Line. The turnaround from the Giuliani administration's perspective could not have been more dramatic.

We decided to announce all these things together: we had a design team, more than $43 million, and virtually all the stakeholders had signed on to the project. It would be the first mayoral press conference on the High Line, but I wasn't going to be there. I used to go several times a year to a Radical Faerie commune in Tennessee, called Short Mountain. I thought, They don't need me at the press conference. It's for the mayor and Gifford. I can go to Short Mountain. Phil called me up and said, "That's crazy. You have to be there."

JOSH

The State's signing on to the railbanking application was part of a package of projects the City and the State were working on jointly, including the Olympic bid, plans to renovate the Javits

Center, and the extension of the number 7 subway line. The stadium sat at the center of it all.

A lot of people were increasingly unhappy with our position on the stadium, or our lack of one. At a party one evening, a friend from college started yelling at me that I was selling out, and that when the stadium was built, it should have my name on it, so that everybody could sit in traffic underneath it and be pissed off at me. The nuances of our position didn't interest him in the least.

ROBERT

Open House New York was going be a bigger event in its second year. We still couldn't invite the public up onto the High Line. But we found a viewing site at the corner of Washington and Gansevoort, where there was an old meatpacking plant. The City's Economic Development Corporation, or EDC, owned the building. They were keeping it vacant as they considered what to do with the property.

The EDC representative in charge, Jeff Manzer, told us that the previous tenants had just up and left one day and never come back. The electricity had been shut off, the refrigeration had stopped, and the meat inside it had rotted. By the time the EDC came to open the building, the stench was unbearable, and the whole place was a foot deep in maggots.

The EDC had cleaned it by the time we got there, but *cleaned* was a relative word. The paint was peeling, everything was rusty, and the place smelled of old meat. There were racks of hooks in the ceiling, and the floors all had drains in them, for blood. There was one room—the refrigerator room—that you didn't dare enter. But if you pushed past all this, on the third floor, you could go through a door to an exterior loading dock with a view of the High Line.

We had to get a City occupancy permit, and our staff and volunteers had to lead people through in groups. As with so much of the project, we relied on the Internet to get the word out. Although I had some background in online marketing, increasingly we relied on Robert Greenhood, a new media and tech expert who built our website and directed our online strategy.

As the day progressed, a long line formed, stretching all the way down Washington Street and around the corner, onto Little West Twelfth Street. People were happily waiting for an hour or more to come up through this old building to get a two-minute glimpse through a chain-link fence at some weeds growing on the High Line. The High Line was becoming more than the High Line. It was becoming a symbol of some kind.

Raise the Money

JOSH

After all those times saying, "If we can't raise the money for a brochure/lawyer/economic study/lobbyist, we'll never be able to raise the money to build the High Line," now we had to raise some private money to build the High Line.

The City had raised its funding allocations to $61 million, but that wasn't going to be enough. Back in 2002 we had estimated that the High Line would cost $65 million to build, but that estimate was based on a far simpler plan than the design team was now working on.

We were trying to bring some federal funding to the project. I'd spent the past year working on an application for $3 million in funding from a program called Congestion Mitigation and Air Quality, or CMAQ. At the same time, Congressman Nadler had made a request of $5 million in the early rounds of the multiyear transportation bill, and our supporters were sending letters to Senators Schumer and Clinton asking them to try to increase that figure when the bill went to the Senate. But even if the federal allocation went up to $10 million, it still wouldn't be enough.

We started talking with our board members about a capital campaign in the area of $50 million. Traditionally it falls to the board to give and to raise the money. It wasn't a discussion that thrilled them at the start. But we'd always said in our proposals that Friends of the High Line would contribute private funding to the High Line's construction, and if we weren't able to, it would put the project—and our standing with the City— in jeopardy.

Juliet Page, our development director, and Robert began interviewing consultants who could launch and run a campaign, and at the end of 2004 they went to talk to Donald Pels about it. Don and Wendy had been there for us at the start, and had helped us with all our most important projects. Juliet had a special relationship with Don; she could speak easily and frankly to him in a way that Robert and I could not. Don had dropped hints to Juliet that he was ready to make a major gift. Juliet understood that he wanted to help us in a way that was strategic as well as financial. He wanted to show the City that donors didn't just want to support the High Line: they wanted to support Friends of the High Line as the stewards of the High Line—the people who would carry this unlikely project forward into the future.

ROBERT

The night before we went to meet with Don, we had our Christmas party. Scott Skey had hosted our staff for dinner at Caviar Russe, and there I tried a B-52 cocktail for the first time.

B-52s are made with Kahlua, Bailey's Irish Cream, and Grand Marnier, and I had several of them. The next morning, on the cab ride up to the Upper East Side, I had to open the door a few times at red lights to throw up.

I met Juliet at a coffee shop. While I pulled myself together, Juliet coached me on what to say. In addition to being hungover, I was also nervous. But Don made Juliet and me feel very relaxed. He knew the drill and practically took us by the hand and led us through it.

JOSH

The envelope landed on my desk, and I opened it. Inside I found Don's check, which had been written out by hand, like the ones you write to pay the phone bill. It was for $1 million, which made me scream.

Juliet was on vacation. I knew she had been anxiously waiting for news from Don, so I called her in Miami. I tortured her a bit, giving her a lot of mundane office details, and then I said, "Oh yeah, by the way, an envelope from Donald Pels arrived." She screamed, too, when I told her what was inside it.

Once again, Don and Wendy had done something incredible for us. Their gift validated the capital campaign for everybody else. Maybe raising $50 million was not such an absurd idea after all.

We have had the good fortune of receiving many other big donations after Don's, donations that made crucial aspects of the High Line possible. Would those gifts have come to us if Don had not stepped up? I don't know. Someone has to step up first. In this case it was Don.

ROBERT

The application for the Certificate of Interim Trail Use required complex negotiations between the City's lawyers, the railroad's lawyers, and our lawyers at Covington and Burling, where Carolyn Corwin had taken over the case from Mike Hemmer. At the same time, as the West Chelsea rezoning progressed, all the twenty-two underlying property owners had to be persuaded to drop their objections to the High Line if the rezoning were to go forward.

JOSH

We were lucky to have Marc Ricks working to get the support of the property owners. Before taking over from Laurel Blatchford at City Hall, Marc had been a consultant with McKinsey and Company. I wasn't sure how much he cared about the High Line during the design team selection. He had a boyish quality that kept you from noticing how smart and determined he was. Marc turned out to be one of the High Line's greatest allies. He had been given a goal by Dan Doctoroff, and he pursued it with a single-minded focus.

As the meetings around the zoning and the Certificate of Interim Trail Use increased in number, we saw Joe Gunn more often. Joe was an attorney in the City's Law Department. When Giuliani was mayor, it had been Joe Gunn's signature at the bottom of the demolition paperwork for the High Line. I'd never met him back then, but I'd hated him abstractly, this invisible Joe Gunn who was bringing the power of the City to bear to take down the High Line. But now Joe Gunn was a real person, a nice guy who was bringing that same power to save the High Line. More than once he and his Law Department colleague Howard Friedman worked through the night to get crucial papers done for the rezoning or for the CITU. Joe would joke that he had to see the High Line through to the end because he couldn't face the prospect of yet another mayor coming in and reversing the policy, as if such a dramatic turnaround could happen again.

ROBERT

The design team was on an ambitious time line to complete plans for the first section. We thought we'd start by building from Gansevoort Street to Fifteenth Street—it's all we had money for. To oversee the designers, we established a working group, with representatives from the City and Friends of the High Line.

We'd usually meet at the architects' offices. I loved going there. Diller Scofidio + Renfro have since moved into large, airy offices at the Starrett-Lehigh Building, overlooking the High Line, but back then they were in a small space just above the Bowery, across from Cooper Union. It was so cluttered with models and stacks of plans that you could barely walk through it. I was convinced that a few of the staff were living there. In contrast, the office of James Corner Field Operations, the landscape architects who were leading the design team, was very spare. It was in the Garment District, and each person's desk there looked like a minimalist artwork.

The principals at both firms had assigned a staff member to oversee the project. At Diller Scofidio + Renfro, Matthew Johnson handled it. At Field Operations, it was Lisa Switkin. Lisa had worked on a submission for the first ideas competition at Grand Central, and after that she had encouraged James Corner to put a team together and enter the competition to design the High Line.

JOSH

At one time, I'd wanted to be an architect. Now I realized I was happier being the client. The High Line architects worked all-nighters, one day after the next, to get it done. Once, I came back from a weekend on Fire Island with a tan and felt terrible when I learned that they had not left the office for days. When they presented their work to us, we would tear it apart. They called us a multiheaded client, because we had people from Parks, City Planning, EDC, and Friends of the High Line each telling them to do something different.

Some of the longest discussions were about the width of the paths and the ratio of hard walking surface to planted area. James Corner argued for keeping the path as narrow as possible. If the planted areas were to dwindle, he said, the High Line would feel like just a path with some bits of planting at the edges. We eventually settled on a minimum path width of about eight feet—enough for a maintenance vehicle and a visitor in a wheelchair to pass each other if they came from opposite directions. At first, I didn't take the issue as seriously as James did, but now, when I walk on the High Line, I see how right he was.

ROBERT

When we talked to the people at the Promenade Plantée, in Paris, they told us that they had made a mistake in not providing more seating. They thought people would use the Promenade Plantée to get from one place to another, but it turned out that people liked to sit and relax. We thought it would probably be the same with the High Line.

The designers didn't want to clutter the High Line with furniture, so they came up with a plan that would allow planks in the walkway to swoop up and become seating—the team called them "peel-up" benches. Originally they were going to be made entirely out of concrete, with no support on the floating end. But to be buildable, they needed support on both ends, so the team devised a steel leg that was virtually invisible. When we told them that concrete would be uncomfortable, they revised the design to make the benches out of wood. They'd originally designed them without backrests, too, but there's a City code that requires half the benches in parks to have back support, so the team revised the plan again to create backrests. During the competition process, we'd thought of this design team as avant-garde, but they showed a real sense of practicality.

The width of the benches, however, was something we didn't want to compromise. The City code for benches in public spaces requires them to be eighteen inches deep, but the seats of our benches were to be an extension of concrete planks that were just twelve inches wide. We tried bulking up the seats, but they didn't look right. In the end, Amanda Burden came up and tried out one of the skinny benches, and she liked them. She saw how clunky they looked when we padded them to make them deeper, and she gave us an exemption.

JOSH

It was a Department of Transportation requirement for bridges and elevated walkways over city streets to have eight-foot-high fences at all the crossings. Some people called it the Frozen Turkey rule, after a famous case of some kids who dropped a frozen turkey from a bridge over a highway onto a moving car below.

To conform to the rule, the design team created a lot of fence options, but the working group started to worry that fences at the street crossings were going to be a big negative. So Peter Mullan did a survey of bridges and elevated walkways in New York City where an eight-foot-high fence had never been installed—places such as the promenade in Brooklyn Heights and the walkway over the Brooklyn Bridge. He also assessed traffic levels at various street crossings beneath the High Line. Then the design team created alternatives to the fences that would ensure safety, without blocking the views.

ROBERT

On the Northern Spur, which crosses Tenth Avenue, the team recommended a landscape preserve, inaccessible to visitors, so that we wouldn't have to put fencing on the historic Art Deco railings there. At a point they were calling Tenth Avenue Square, which floats right over the avenue, with traffic streaming underneath, the team proposed to bring visitors down into the structure, so that the High Line itself would form its own eight-foot-high barrier. It's an example of how the constraints on the project led to some of its iconic features.

JOSH

Adrian Benepe, the parks commissioner, surprised us with his enthusiasm for the design team's more ambitious ideas. The Parks Department has to maintain many parks, and they've come up with standardized systems that make this easier, such as pathways made of "hex pavers"—six-sided cement tiles that can be easily installed and replaced. Some Parks Department staff members had argued for these traditional treatments on the High Line. But when the designs came up to Adrian at our steering committee meetings, Adrian said, "The High Line is going to be much more than a park. It is going to be a work of art."

ROBERT

The ideas exhibition at Grand Central had greatly increased our visibility, and I wanted to exhibit the team's preliminary design work in a similar way, maybe in one of the West Chelsea galleries. It was Juliet who said, "Let's have it at MoMA."

The Museum of Modern Art had been closed for renovations for several years, and it was getting ready to reopen. Juliet said,

"Why don't you call Terry Riley? Maybe he'll exhibit the High Line design right when the museum reopens." I told her it would never happen. But Juliet kept harping on it. So I e-mailed Terry, who ran MoMA's architecture and design department: "I know this is a crazy idea, but I just wanted to run it past you." He wrote right back: "Great idea, let's do it."

The show opened in April. It was supposed to run for three months, but it was so popular that MoMA kept it up for six.

In the center of the room, a model of the High Line, from Gansevoort Street to Fifteenth Street, was suspended from the ceiling. Three walls were covered in boards that presented the design, and on the fourth wall we projected a video that had been made with time-lapse stills, which took the viewer on a walk up the High Line from south to north. Next to the projection, we hung several of Joel Sternfeld's photographs of the High Line, and if you followed these into the next room, they brought you to a model of Steven Holl's "Bridge of Houses," which was in the MoMA's collection. Seeing the visions of Holl, Sternfeld, and the design team all together gave you a sense of the project evolving over time.

Hundreds of thousands of people saw the exhibition. For a long time afterward, if I began to talk to someone about the High Line, they would instantly say, "I saw the show at MoMA."

The MoMA exhibit was a symbolic step, too. It didn't change anything about the legal, political, or financial hurdles that lay ahead. But once we were at MoMA, people thought the High Line was definitely going to happen.

Dan Doctoroff came to the opening party. It was a particularly tough time for the stadium plan. Cablevision, which owned Madison Square Garden, was running a barrage of TV ads against the stadium, which would compete with its sports and concert businesses. We'd dodged the stadium issue in the exhibition, truncating the map of the High Line at Eleventh Avenue and Thirtieth Street, leaving out the western rail yards entirely. I was nervous about seeing Dan at the party. He had brought us so far, and we weren't backing him up.

JOSH

The meatpacking building we'd used for Open House New York, 820 Washington Street, was still vacant. It sat on the corner of a City-owned block that was almost entirely occupied by meatpackers. The High Line ran right through the building before ending at Gansevoort Street.

We hoped to secure part of the 820 Washington site to build stairs and an elevator to the High Line, but we weren't the only ones with designs on the building. Woolco, a food wholesaler that had been displaced by the new Theory flagship clothing store, wanted the building, too. They'd threatened to move their business to New Jersey if they didn't get a low rent from the City.

Jim Capalino introduced me to James Ortenzio. Jim said Ortenzio knew the Woolco guys. Ortenzio was a famous character in the Meatpacking District. If Florent was the mayor of everything hip and fashionable in the area, Ortenzio was the mayor of everything else: the meatpackers, the longtime property owners, all the people who came there before the fashionable shops. He owned a building on Washington Street that he rented to a meat business for almost nothing—just because he liked the guys.

My first meeting with Ortenzio was a breakfast at Hector's, the old-time diner under the High Line at the corner of Little West Twelfth and Washington. In between allusions to Roman battles, Latin phrases, and a story about speaking a remote Austrian dialect and trading swords—not barbs, but actual swords—with Arnold Schwarzenegger, Ortenzio let me know he thought providing access to the new High Line was a neighborhood priority and that he would make sure Woolco agreed. In the end, Woolco moved to New Jersey, so it wasn't an issue. But now I knew Ortenzio. I often had no idea what he was talking about, but I quickly learned to take his advice.

Ortenzio made sure that access for the High Line would be a given in any new proposals for 820 Washington. Jo Hamilton, from Save Gansevoort Market, was hoping to make a flower market in the building. Meatpackers in the neighborhood also wanted the building. And Phil Aarons told me that Michael Govan, the executive director of Dia Center for the Arts, was looking for a new Manhattan home for Dia, so I called Michael up and showed him 820 Washington.

Dia's original West Twenty-second Street space had spurred the transformation of West Chelsea. But its small stairs and elevator couldn't accommodate many visitors, and the building had no air-conditioning, so it would close during summer months.

Michael hoped to find a site where a new building could be funded by the sale of the old one. He came to show us his museum proposal, which we liked. It left space free under the High Line for our stairs and elevator, and it included a floor on the High Line level to house our office and maintenance facility. We also liked the spirit of the idea: the art world had supported the High Line from the very start, and we hoped that art would be a major part of the High Line when it opened.

Even if his plan had been a terrible idea, Michael would have won us over. He was blessed with a combination of good looks, intelligence, and charisma that made it impossible to dislike anything he told you. When he came to our office in his tailored

Prada suit, I didn't hear all that much of what he said. I just saw his dark eyes glinting and watched his nice lips opening and closing and thought, Yes. He must have been similarly convincing with others, because by May, Dia's deal with the City was announced in the *Times*.

ROBERT

We were not sure if the meat market guys would want a museum coming to a block that had been previously ruled by the meat industry. Ortenzio convened a breakfast at Florent with me and Michael Govan to work out a proposal that Ortenzio could take back to the meat market guys. Michael was a great talker, but with Ortenzio, he barely got a word in edgewise. Ortenzio kept calling Michael "Agent Jack." It looked like it was going to end badly. But a deal was struck. Michael would reserve half of the bottom floor of the museum for meatpacking. Dia was going to be the museum with meatpacking at one end and the High Line at the other.

JOSH

As the Dia plan was coming to life at the southern end of the High Line, at the northern end the stadium plan was dying. Cablevision's anti-stadium television ads were relentless. At the gym, I'd see them playing across all six screens in front of the StairMasters. They made me angry, because they featured neighborhood people criticizing the plan but they had been paid for by a big private company that had a corporate interest in blocking the stadium. And they worked. They took a localized community opposition and blasted it citywide.

An obscure State agency dealt the final blow. The Public Authorities Control Board refused to authorize the State's financial contribution to the stadium. This meant that it could not be included in the City's 2012 Olympic bid package. Without the Olympics behind it, the stadium didn't stand a chance.

In our office, the general feeling was one of relief. A public controversy that had been very difficult for us was finally over. I was a little disappointed, though I never said it at the time. Whether you liked it or not, the stadium was a bold vision, and it had gone down.

Railbanked!

ROBERT

The final push for the rezoning started in May 2005, leading up to a City Council hearing on June 15. We worked to bring a large group of supporters to City Hall in green High Line T-shirts—with a graphic of hands making a heart around the High Line logo—the day of the hearing. Gifford, as the speaker, and Christine Quinn, as the local council member, were both voicing strong support for the parts of the plan that supported reuse of the High Line, and we wanted to back them up.

During the rezoning process, there were many competing constituencies. Nobody got everything they wanted, but in the end everybody's issues were addressed. Christine's office and City Planning and the Department of Housing Preservation and Development worked to increase the incentives for developers to include affordable housing in new buildings. Preservationists were promised a study for a new historic district, which would regulate development between Twenty-fifth and Twenty-seventh streets, where a group of large, handsome prewar warehouses were located. An agreement was made with 32BJ, the union that represents porters, maintenance workers, and doormen: the doormen in any buildings in the new district would have to be unionized. And the underlying property owners won the right to sell their development rights above the High Line to sites along Tenth and Eleventh avenues. The height restrictions were kept low near the Chelsea Historic District, but greater allowances were made at its north and south ends.

Even though the City Council hadn't voted yet, the rezoning looked so likely that, several weeks before the hearing, the property owners filed with the Surface Transportation Board withdrawing their long-standing objections to the High Line. This removed the final objection to railbanking. On June 13, just two days before the City Council hearing, we got the news that the STB had approved the City's application for a Certificate of Interim Trail Use.

JOSH

We'd been pursuing the CITU for more than five years. We originally thought we could just apply and get one, the way you'd send away for a prize by mailing in a couple of cereal box tops. We had no idea what it would actually take.

ROBERT

The news landed on the front page of the *Times*: a color photo with the caption "Frog of a Railroad to Become Prince of a Park."

JOSH

At the June 15 hearing in the Council Chamber at City Hall, Amanda had to restrain herself. She clutched the newspaper in her hands. She was practically shaking with joy.

ROBERT

The CITU's coming through and the rezoning, just days apart, were two huge wins for us. But our excitement at these victories was always tempered by the knowledge of how much we still had to do: raising the money, finishing the design, building it. We'd always tried to present a face that led people to believe that everything was going really, really well. But Josh and I both were always looking over our shoulders.

JOSH

Our summer benefit was just a few weeks later. Barbaralee Diamonstein-Spielvogel got us a deal at Cipriani Wall Street. We had to pay only fifty dollars per head because someone at Cipriani owed Barbaralee a favor.

Cipriani Wall Street had once been the U.S. Custom House. You felt dwarfed when you walked into the hall, which had been designed by McKim, Mead and White. I whispered to Juliet, "We'll never fill this place." But we did: we had nine hundred guests seated for dinner. A friend of Robert's had introduced us to CNN's Anderson Cooper, who agreed to be master of ceremonies. We had benefit honorees for the first time: Amanda Burden, Joel Sternfeld, and Ed Norton, Sr., the father of Edward Norton; Ed Senior had been a founding board member at the Rails-to-Trails Conservancy.

We raised more than $1 million that night. It was the first time we'd raised so much at a dinner. As the lights went down, a video played detailing our run of recent victories—the rezoning, the CITU, plans for Dia at the base of the High Line, the exhibition at MoMA. With each of these announcements, the whole room roared.

Many of the underlying property owners who had originally opposed us bought tables that night, including Jerry Gottesman, once the leader of the demolition effort. Joe Rose bought a table, too. As the planning chair before Amanda, he had been the face of the Giuliani administration's anti–High Line policy. Now his real estate company had an option on a major development site next to the High Line. Toward the end of the evening, as I squeezed my way down the crowded staircase from the mezzanine to the main floor, I saw Joe Rose coming up the stairs toward me. Smiling, he reached out and took my hand and pulled me into one of those warm, awkward handshakes that is also partly a hug. He said, "You guys have done an incredible job." I knew a page had turned.

ROBERT

Senator Clinton came to the High Line that August to announce $18 million in federal funding for the High Line in the reauthorization of the multiyear transportation bill. This was the allocation that Congressman Nadler had started with a

$5 million request in the House. When the bill moved to the Senate, Clinton and Schumer had been able to raise it to $18 million. Many of our supporters had advocated for this funding, from the hundreds of volunteers who wrote letters to both the senators, to board members such as Barbaralee, who knew the political players well.

JOSH

It was over ninety degrees when Senator Clinton arrived. I was drenched in sweat as we walked through the sun-frazzled weeds of the High Line. Senator Clinton, properly coiffed, in a suit, did not sweat a bit.

ROBERT

Shortly before the exhibition closed, at the end of October, we went to MoMA with Diane von Furstenberg and Barry Diller. Alex von Furstenberg, who'd recently joined our board, was encouraging them to get more involved. The principals of the design team, James Corner, Ric Scofidio, and Liz Diller, came along to walk them through the exhibition.

JOSH

The year 2005 marked the twentieth anniversary of the restaurant Florent; its owner, Florent Morellet, had come to the Meatpacking District in 1985. We adored Florent and wanted to celebrate his restaurant with a fun event that would bring some funds to the High Line and the Meatpacking District Initiative, a neighborhood group headed by our friend Annie Washburn.

Florent doesn't do anything small, and we must have considered twenty different bars, clubs, garages, and galleries before we settled on the Roxy, on Eighteenth and Eleventh.

Florent named the event "Florent's Bi-Decade(nt) Ball and Miss Meat Market Gown Contest." Friends of the High Line handled the administrative side, and Florent curated the performances, bringing in Flotilla DeBarge and Murray Hill as MCs and a roster of performers. The first drama came when the Roxy booked a "secret" performance by Madonna right after our event. This meant that the charming fellows at the Roxy—who had threatened to kill us, literally, if we mentioned anything about their "secret" performance in our promotions—were going to kick out all our guests early in the evening to make room for the Madonna people. Our invitations had been mailed, there was little we could do about it, and word leaked out about Madonna online, so we tried to harness the "secret" performance for what it was worth, and a lot of people did buy tickets to our event thinking they'd be allowed to stay for Madonna.

Robert and I had eagerly agreed to dress in drag in the Miss Meat Market Gown Contest. By the time we came out of the green room, only Dirty Martini remained onstage, doing her remarkable pasty-spinning routine, making her boobs spin the pasties one way, then the other, and then back again. Robert was eliminated fairly early from the gown contest. That's what happens when you don't practice walking in heels. I made it to third runner-up. Diller Scofidio + Renfro had outfitted their model in a dress made of very thinly sliced meat—prosciutto, maybe—this was years ahead of Lady Gaga's meat dress. But the thin meat went oily under the lights, and she was eliminated.

Shortly after the contest, the Roxy people herded our guests out of the club and into a thundering rainstorm. We huddled under the High Line, whose failed drainage system created a kind of Niagara Falls outside the Roxy's front door. Still in our makeup, we ended up at Billy's Bakery on Ninth Avenue, and it was only then that I learned what had happened while Robert and I were getting our lashes glued on: A noteworthy series of performances had taken place. One of the high points was Julie Atlas Muz, who had lip-synched a Judas Priest song, "Breaking the Law," with her vagina. The next morning, Robert got an e-mail from one of our supporters. It read, "That was a lovely evening. I'm sorry I missed seeing you. But when the man dressed as a priest took the man dressed as an altar boy over his knees, pulled down his pants, and began spanking him, and then pulled a string of rosary beads out of his ass, I thought it was my cue to leave."

For weeks after that, I waited for the other shoe to drop. There would be a scandalized article about the event, and the City would sever their ties with us. After all this, we were going to be undone by the singing vagina and the rosary beads. But the article never ran, and the Bloomberg administration continued to view us as acceptable partners.

ROBERT

Anne Pasternak was the executive director of Creative Time, which does site-specific public art installations. Amanda Burden had been her board chair for many years, and Phil was also on the board; he had introduced Anne to me. Anne came on one of our very first walks on the High Line, back in 1999 or 2000, and she'd wanted to do a project with us ever since. We'd showed her the old meatpacking plant at 820 Washington Street, the site that Dia was taking. She loved the building. I discouraged her from working there, because getting approval from the City would be difficult. But she persuaded Jeff Manzer, who still managed the property for EDC, to let her use it. Anne and her curator, Peter Eleey, brought in fourteen different works and called the show *The Plain of Heaven*. A dancer, performing choreography by William Forsythe, danced on the top floor in the Cutting Room, so named because it's where they used to cut the meat. In another room, Peter Eleey projected a video he had tracked down of Gordon Matta-Clark's 1975 cutting project on Pier 52, which was located directly across the West Side Highway. The footage showed pieces of the old pier shed being cut away, allowing the sun to pour in. Many of the entries to the High Line's ideas competition had referred to Matta-Clark's work, proposing cuttings into the High Line—and the stairs our design team was proposing followed this idea.

JOSH

"RAILBANKED!" We set the letters in full caps over one of Joel Sternfeld's photographs and mailed it to our supporters. It was official now. After securing the Certificate of Interim Trail Use, the City and CSX Transportation had negotiated a Trail Use Agreement, which formalized the High Line's future as a park. At the same time, CSX donated the High Line south of Thirtieth Street to the City. Nothing more stood in our way. We could break ground.

The one wrinkle was that CSX would retain ownership of the High Line north of Thirtieth Street, around the rail yards. With the stadium gone and that piece of the High Line out of the agreements, it was easier to bring all parties to consensus. No one knew what would happen at that site, but for now we had two-thirds of the High Line locked in.

"I Saved the High Line"

JOSH

After their visit to the MoMA exhibition, we sent a proposal for funding to Diane von Furstenberg, Barry Diller, and Alex von Furstenberg. Having deliberated with Barry and the family for a few months, Diane asked Robert and me to come to her office. She wanted to let us know what they'd decided.

You prepare yourself to be disappointed in meetings like this. The gift someone has decided on might be much less than what you hoped for, and you need to be ready to be effusively grateful nonetheless.

Diane's office was on West Twelfth Street, on the top floor of the stable/carriage house complex where she had hosted parties for us in the past. It was more like a fabulous apartment than an office, decorated in earthy, lipstick colors, with stacks of art and fashion books, Balinese carvings, and personal photos. Pinned to a board on one wall were shots of Alex; his sister, Tatiana; and Diane at various ages and at various sunny places. There was also a framed photo I remembered having seen in *Vanity Fair*, shot by Annie Leibovitz, of Barry and Diane posed on a pale silk couch in an apartment in the Carlyle Hotel.

When Diane came in, she sat us down and asked us how the project was going. Then she leaned forward, forearms on her knees, and said, "Listen, guys, we want to do five."

The "five" was $5 million. All the numbers we'd proposed were in millions. We'd dared to hope it might be five, but we'd prepared ourselves to be thankful for much less. I was so happy I could have started crying right there. I don't remember the rest of the meeting, just returning to the office and the cheer that erupted there.

ROBERT

Christine Quinn was elected as speaker of the City Council in January 2006, after Gifford had term-limited out. When Gifford first campaigned for speaker, people had said we'd never have a speaker from Manhattan. Now Christine was another council member from Manhattan, and an out-of-the-closet gay woman. Like Gifford before her, Christine had campaigned strategically, built strong relationships in Brooklyn and Queens, and secured the votes she needed from her colleagues.

JOSH

I was proud of Christine and proud to live in New York City, which had made this strong woman its first openly gay speaker of the City Council—the most powerful position in City government, other than mayor.

We had expected that having both sides of City Hall supporting the High Line would end when Gifford left office, but our good fortune would be extended. The High Line was in Christine's district, there was no council member more supportive, and now she was speaker.

ROBERT

Construction workers started going up in February.

Some people see the High Line and think we just laid the concrete planks down on top of the existing landscape, but we had to remove everything first. We had to get down to the concrete slab that held the gravel ballast, to make repairs and put in a new drainage system. The drainage hadn't worked for decades. It's one of the reasons people complained about the High Line. It leaked on them.

The site preparation work was the most expensive thing about the project. Removing the original lead paint and repainting all the steel was one of the costliest parts of all—$16.4 million.

JOSH

The removals began with the lifting of equipment. We'd look out our office windows and see a bulldozer floating through the air, suspended from a crane.

During the six years we'd been working on the High Line, it was always empty, except for the occasional trespasser. Now, as

I walked to work along Fourteenth Street, I could look up and see contractors in hard hats and fluorescent safety vests. The project we thought would never happen had started to happen.

ROBERT

First, the contractors painted yellow numbers on the steel railroad tracks, tagging them according to a site survey, so we could reinstall any rail in its original location. You can still see the numbers on some of the reinstalled tracks in the park. After the rails were lifted and stored, the workers started scraping everything else away. As they dug, you realized how fragile the plant life was. It was just a thin layer, just inches deep, rooted in the gravel ballast. It astounded me that such a lush landscape could grow in virtually no soil.

Taking it all away was bittersweet, because there was no going back. As much as I loved the design our team had made, my fear was that it wouldn't compare with what was there already. But you could keep that original landscape only if no one went up there.

JOSH

It was brutal to see it ripped up. They cut a big hole out of the High Line, and the bulldozers shoved that gorgeous Joel Sternfeld landscape down through it. Katie Lorah, who'd joined our staff as an office assistant, and who was gradually taking over our press relations, took videos of all the gravel and rail ties and other debris cascading down into truck beds below.

ROBERT

The plants were so hardy. There were areas where we'd stop working for some reason, and the plants would immediately start colonizing the place again, growing out of the mountains of bulldozed gravel.

JOSH

For a while it was just a torn-up mess of mud and gravel and muck, and then they got it down to the bare, clean concrete. It became a blank slate, which felt liberating. It freed you from thinking of the High Line purely as something to be preserved, and it allowed you to focus on what you could create there.

ROBERT

We hosted a community input forum on the design at Cedar Lake, a dance space on West Twenty-sixth Street, around the same time as the start of construction. It was our third—we'd done one right after the ideas competition, and another after the design team was selected.

We made a point of taking the design team into the community regularly. Designers often don't like to do this early in the process. They don't want the community to reject their ideas before they can develop them fully and present them in their best light, with renderings and models. But you don't have to do everything the community suggests. If you go back and say, "We heard what you said, but we're going in this other direction and this is why," they often appreciate your reasoning and that you listened.

People said they didn't want people on bikes up there, and they didn't want it to have lots of commercial activity. The design team had come up with a slogan to define their approach: Keep it simple, keep it wild, keep it quiet, keep it slow. Most of what we heard from the community supported that idea.

JOSH

Jennifer Falk in the mayor's press office was our partner on the groundbreaking ceremony in April. Robert and I had strong opinions about the High Line, and we were accustomed to pushing until we got our way, but that didn't work with Jenn: you can't really fight the mayor's press office. So I learned to just do it Jenn's way. It was a good lesson about conceding: her way was usually better than ours.

It was Jenn who said, "You can't do a groundbreaking! You've already bulldozed the place!" Instead, she came up with another idea: the last bit of railroad track remaining in the construction area would be lifted, and all the elected officials could pose behind it for the cameras.

Everybody was going to wear hard hats, except for the officials. After the photo of Michael Dukakis in the tank during the 1988 presidential election, it became a rule in press offices not to put your politician in a hat.

Jenn said, "If I'm going to have all these hard hats in the shot, don't give me white hard hats. Give me hard hats with a color, something that will pop." We ended up with bright green hard hats. The hats each had a simple line drawing of a flower on the front, an iconic image by a street artist named Michael De Feo. Michael used to wheat-paste copies of this flower all over New York City, often on the bases of streetlamps. The flower had a childlike, optimistic feel that was just right for the ceremony.

The groundbreaking was held on a beautiful, sunny April morning. From the podium, we faced hundreds of supporters in our bright green hats with the cheerful flower. The crowd's happiness for us and for the project felt even greater than our own. You could feel it beaming up at you.

Along with all the government officials who'd been supporting the project, Barry Diller and Diane von Furstenberg were at the podium with us to announce their $5 million gift. Of all the speeches that day, and there were many, the words I remember are Diane's. She said, "The High Line tells us that in New York City dreams come true."

ROBERT

The hundreds of people who were up on the High Line with us that day, and a thousand more at a party down on the street, were all wearing little buttons that read, "I Saved the High Line." Most of them really had saved it. Thousands of people had helped make it happen.

In my favorite photo from the rail lift, all the officials have their hands on the rail that's being lifted—Christine Quinn, Hillary Clinton, Chuck Schumer, Mayor Bloomberg, Amanda Burden, and Jerry Nadler. They're all looking in different directions; none of them is looking at the others.

Gifford wasn't up on the podium; he was in the audience. That was our mistake. By then he wasn't speaker anymore, but we could have fought for him to be up there. He never said anything about it, but he should have been up there with us.

JOSH

The design team was protective of the High Line, and they didn't want mundane aspects of everyday life diluting its special qualities. For example, they argued against people being able to get a cup of coffee on the High Line, because there are a million other places in New York to drink coffee. You could see their perspective in their original designs for connections to the buildings alongside the High Line. They were like drawbridges, a guarded stance on the idea of connection.

Amanda Burden, too, was concerned about differentiating the experience of the High Line from that of life below. If you had too many doors opening onto it, the High Line would become just another city street. And nobody wanted doors from private buildings to make the High Line feel exclusive. In New York City, there is no tradition of private properties enjoying private access to public parks, and we didn't want to start one.

At the same time, what if we built the High Line and no one came? We might need people to come from adjacent buildings for the park to feel safe and welcoming. This followed the Jane Jacobs line of thought about what makes parks successful: diverse groups of visitors coming from diverse places for different reasons at different times of day.

The arrival of the Caledonia on the scene forced our hand. The Caledonia, which was going up on West Seventeenth Street, was the first residential development to be built next to the High Line under the provisions of the West Chelsea rezoning. The developers, The Related Companies, were asking for a connection.

Friends of the High Line worked with City Planning and the Parks Department to come up with a policy that would serve the public first and foremost, and at the same time meet the demand from building residents. Put simply, there would be no private doors from private buildings onto the High Line. If you were a developer who wanted to connect a building to the High Line, you first had to build a fully public vertical access system, including both stairs and elevator, that would allow the public to go up to the High Line from the sidewalk. You could then put a door to your building into that public vertical access system, so that people from the building would mix with the general public and then everyone would step onto the High Line together. You would also have to pay an annual fee to the City for the right to this connection. The fee would go to a special City-controlled fund to support the High Line.

The Caledonia had already designed a public stair and elevator as part of their building, so it was relatively simple for them to design a door connecting the building with the stairway. But the door has never been opened. The Caledonia and the City could never agree on the fee.

As time goes on, it looks like connections like these will rarely, if ever, happen. From the developers' side, the security issues are complex: a connection represents one more security point within a building that has to be manned. From the High Line's perspective, we have the good fortune of having many more visitors than we expected, and so the main reason for considering connections is not very strong.

ROBERT

The Caledonia was under construction almost as soon as the rezoning passed. At twenty-six stories, it was one of the larger buildings that the rezoning allowed.

Usually when you market a building like this, you show a rendering of it. But in this case, full-page ads ran in *The New York Times Magazine* and *New York* magazine, showing just a detail of the High Line's Art Deco railing. The ads said the Caledonia would be the first luxury condominium on the High Line. They were using proximity to the High Line to sell apartments. Even though we had predicted in the economic feasibility study that this might happen, it was surprising to see it actually happen.

JOSH

About a month after the rail lift, the mayor hosted a cultivation dinner to introduce the High Line to new donors who might support the $50 million capital campaign. We wanted to have the dinner in a space with a view of the High Line, so we went back to the Phillips de Pury auction house, which looked over the High Line between Fourteenth and Fifteenth streets, with the river in the background.

By then John Blondel had joined our board. John, who worked at Goldman Sachs, teamed up with two Goldman colleagues, David Heller and Jen Padovani, to come up with a list of people to invite to the Mayor's dinner. They weren't aiming at the titans who were already on nonprofit boards with buildings named after them, but at smart, up-and-coming people, many of them in finance, the young stars of an economy that was peaking—though, at the time, we didn't know it was peaking. We started the evening with a tour of the construction site, and then everyone came to dinner at Phillips.

After the mayor spoke, he opened the floor for questions. Joel Sternfeld had become increasingly passionate about environmental issues, and he grilled the mayor on his environmental policies, asking him if he would make a green roof on City Hall. The mayor's first answer didn't satisfy Joel, so Joel kept challenging him, and the two of them parried back and forth. It made the dinner less like a mayoral event and more like a dinner party.

Some of the guests went on to become some of the High Line's most valued supporters, including David and Hermine Heller, Mike and Sukey Novogratz, Bill and Karen Ackman, and Philip and Lisa Falcone.

ROBERT

Safely removing the lead paint from the High Line and repainting it was the most expensive part of the construction contract. The structure had been painted just twice since the 1930s, once in a reddish-brown color, and once in a darker brown, closer to black. Very little of the original paint remained. The color most people associated with the High Line was rust. Ideally, the color we painted it would make it seem that it had been there always, that nothing had changed. We tested swatches of about fifteen different colors at a crossing at West Thirteenth Street. Together they looked like Neapolitan ice cream. Amanda Burden visited several times to consider them, looking at them from the street and then going up the construction stairs to view them up close. Nothing looked right: the reddish browns were muddy; the light tan seemed out of place. Black seemed the cleanest, but we worried it would be foreboding. The design team went back and researched a modified black, and found a color we all agreed on: "Greenblack." This is exactly what it sounds like: black with such a slight tint of green that you don't really see it. Sherwin-Williams makes it. Anyone can get it. I recently went to the hardware store and bought some to paint my kitchen. The number to ask for is SW6994.

JOSH

In June, as the City's budget was being finalized, Manhattan borough president Scott Stringer announced a $2 million allocation to the High Line. The previous winter, Gifford, as the outgoing speaker, had invited Scott, the incoming borough president, to visit the High Line. Gifford was late, so I took Scott up for the tour. It was a brutally cold day. The High Line was covered in a layer of ice, and Scott slipped and skidded along in his leather-soled dress shoes, doing his best to suggest enthusiasm. Gifford arrived just as Scott was leaving. Scott said, "Thanks for the great invitation, Gifford. So glad you decided to show up." But he saw past this lousy first impression to what the High Line could mean for the city. Between his allocation, the out-year allocations Gifford had made, and contributions to the project made by the Mayor's Office, the scope of what we were building in the first round of construction could be expanded. We weren't stopping at Fifteenth Street anymore. We were going all the way to Twentieth Street.

ROBERT

Michael Govan surprised everyone by leaving Dia to take the top job at the Los Angeles County Museum of Art. Then, a few months after he left, Dia's board chair, Len Riggio, the CEO of Barnes and Noble, stepped down, too. Having lost both its chair and its director, in the fall of 2006, Dia dropped its plans to build at the High Line site.

We were worried about what would take Dia's place, but we didn't have to worry for long. Within a week, the Whitney Museum of American Art announced that it wanted to build on the site. It had been attempting to expand its Madison Avenue building for years. It had abandoned one expansion plan, designed by Michael Graves, in 1985, and another, designed by Rem Koolhaas, in 2003. More recently, it had been working with Renzo Piano to advance a third expansion plan, but it faced vehement community opposition—it seemed that every other week there was a story in the *Times* about the Whitney's battles with the Friends of the Upper East Side Historic District. It made more sense to start over on a new site.

Adam Weinberg, the Whitney's director, was down at our office within days. He brought Renzo Piano to meet with us a few weeks later. Adam was happy to be working in a neighborhood where the community embraced the project, and we were happy that we would have a major art museum anchoring the southern end of the High Line.

JOSH

In October we brought a group of volunteers up to the northern part of the High Line, above the construction site, to harvest seeds from native plants so that we could replant them in the park after construction. Staff from the Parks Department's Greenbelt Native Plant Center, on Staten Island, taught our volunteers which seeds to harvest, and at the end of the day the seeds were sent back to the Native Plant Center, where they were dried and stored in a seed archive. The volunteers collected enough seeds that day to fill thirty-five large bags, from plants such as purple lovegrass, evening primrose, and tall thoroughwort.

It was a crisp, clear fall day, and there was something restorative about being up on the High Line with so many cheerful volunteers, collecting the seeds that could bring a piece of the original landscape back to life.

Rail Yards

ROBERT

With the stadium plans gone, the City's Hudson Yards Development Corporation, or HYDC, began a revised planning effort, and it didn't look good for the High Line. The High Line was positioned as this thing that was nice but was too expensive to keep.

The rail yards were made up of two sites, the eastern and the western rail yards. In the Olympic-oriented planning, the eastern yards were rezoned for a hotel, a cultural center, residences, office space, and parking. This was intended to complement the stadium, which would occupy the western yards. Now the western yards would be entirely rezoned for a mixture of uses to bring the whole plan into alignment.

Planners at HYDC defined the High Line as a matter of cost: it could be kept at the site if it didn't cost too much. Then they said they'd done a study that showed that keeping the High Line would add $120 million in costs to the project. When we actually saw the study, there was nothing backing up this charge—no engineering, no construction analysis. So we set out to do our own studies, examining the planning rationale, the economic benefits, the construction feasibility, and the cost consequences of maintaining the High Line at the rail yards.

It was tough, having to fight to save the High Line all over again. HYDC was going to release a Request for Proposals (RFP) to developers, and the priorities written into this RFP would affect whether a developer proposed keeping the High Line. So we were fighting to get language into a planning document most people had never heard of.

We did our study in two phases. In the first phase, we looked at the planning rationale for keeping the High Line at the rail yards, and its potential economic value. When we presented the promising findings to HYDC, they responded with new challenges. They said the High Line would add unnecessary costs and would physically obstruct construction. Specifically, they needed a really big crane, and there was no way a really big crane could get onto the site with the High Line in the way. So we hired construction managers and cost estimators, and we found that it might actually cost *less* to keep the High Line—you wouldn't have to demolish it, which resulted in a savings. At most it would add between $2 million and $10 million to the total costs, not the $120 million HYDC had estimated. As for the crane, our consultants found that every single thing that's built in Manhattan is constructed with materials and equipment that comes over bridges and through tunnels, and the dimensions under the High Line are no more restrictive than those. I took particular pleasure in projecting up on the screen at the HYDC offices the diagram that showed that the crane the MTA needed would fit easily under the High Line. For every objection they raised, we found an expert who developed a solution.

Once again, we were walking a fine line. HYDC was a City agency, and the City was our partner in the High Line. It was a City priority to get something built at the rail yards that would ultimately be good for New York.

John Alschuler, who did our economic feasibility study back in 2002 and who had since joined our board of directors, did our rail yards studies for us. He was passionate about it. He is usually very measured in his tone, but I'd never seen him get as upset at government representatives as he was in those meetings with HYDC. It angered him that they would not consider the case on its merits, and he took a stance I never thought I'd see him take. He said, "We'll do everything in our power to stop you. You'll never build Hudson Yards over our opposition. If you do build it, we'll make it take ten years longer." John makes his living consulting for the type of development agency he was now threatening. He put his reputation on the line for us.

Josh and I were sometimes ambivalent about this fight, because we had so much work to do to build the southern part of the High Line and to raise the money to run it. But in the end we knew we had to fight for the rail yards section. Phil would say, "We're Friends of the High Line—of the entire High Line. We're not Friends of part of the High Line."

JOSH

The rail yards were State property, and we hoped we could depend on the support of the new governor, Eliot Spitzer, who was sworn in at the start of January 2007. We had better connections to Spitzer than we'd had to Governor Pataki. Barbaralee Diamonstein-Spielvogel had arranged for him to come to our summer benefit the previous year, when he was still campaigning—he had presented awards to Diane von Furstenberg, Kevin Bacon, and Christine Quinn, our three honorees. But it was just the start of Spitzer's administration, and there were other priorities above the High Line on the governor's list. Our hope was that tearing down the High Line at the rail yards would be just too unpopular for this governor, or any elected official, to tolerate.

About four years after she'd joined our staff as our first
development director and first full-time employee, Juliet Page
moved to New Orleans. Her husband had been hired at Tulane.
It was hard to imagine Friends of the High Line without Juliet.
She'd been more than our development director. She'd helped
us shape our mission and our programs. She said that when we
opened the High Line, we would want all sorts of people to feel
a part of it. She got us to pay attention to how we worked with
the community, especially our neighbors in the Fulton and
Chelsea-Elliott houses. She'd encouraged us to bring a diverse
mix of neighbors into the design process, and to start an
education program.

She'd brought with her, from her work at New Yorkers for
Parks, the belief that parks are important because they're places
where everyone in the city meets—rich and poor, from all
different backgrounds and professions.

We did a search for a development director who had completed
a capital campaign. Our campaign was off to a good start, but
there was still a long way to go. Diane Nixa, who was at the New
Jersey Performing Arts Center, in Newark, had completed several
campaigns. She was from Minnesota and had a wide smile and a
no-nonsense approach. There can be a lot of arcane lingo and
pretension in the nonprofit world. Diane cut through that.

Diane joined our staff right after the Mayor's dinner, and she
put together several events to follow it. The first was at the
IAC/InterActiveCorp building.

Barry Diller had commissioned Frank Gehry to design IAC's
new headquarters—Gehry's first big building in New York. We'd
watched from the High Line as its strange form rose along the
West Side Highway. It had a wavy façade of milk-colored glass,
inspired by a ship's sails. Anyone with an interest in architecture
was dying to get inside it. When Barry offered to host a lunch
for our donors as the first event in the new building, we knew it
was a great opportunity.

About fifty people—some guests who'd attended the
Mayor's dinner and others whom Barry and Diane von
Furstenberg had invited—sat on both sides of a long table.
Everything was white—the tablecloth, the flowers, the chairs.
Barry, Robert, and I each spoke. Behind us, renderings of the
special features of the High Line's design were projected on the
massive video wall that ran along the length of the space.

I took the part of asking our guests to consider making a gift.
In the past, Robert had generally done the asking, but I was
teaching myself to do it more. The hardest part at the start was
just getting the words out of my mouth. On the mornings

before big meetings with donors, I would practice on my dog, who would look at me with a tilted head as I asked him for a million dollars over and over again.

ROBERT

After IAC, we did a smaller event at the new offices of Diller Scofidio + Renfro. Edward Norton was the host, and Ric Scofidio, Liz Diller, and Charles Renfro were there to talk about the design. The guests were a small group of people who had shown a growing interest in the High Line: Karen and Bill Ackman, Lisa and Philip Falcone, Hermine and David Heller, Brittany and Adam Levinson, and Sukey and Mike Novogratz. Mike told us that he and Sukey had come to our community event at The Kitchen back in early 2001, but that the High Line had looked like such a long shot back then that they hadn't gotten more involved.

When we showed the rendering of the Tenth Avenue Square, with its amphitheater seating stepping down to the glass panels looking out over the traffic, I could tell it caught Mike's attention. He'd seen Liz Diller speak at a TED conference, and she'd talked about the media room they'd designed for the Institute of Contemporary Art in Boston, which stepped down to a wall of windows overlooking Boston Harbor. Mike could see the relationship between the ICA media room and the Tenth Avenue Square. When we told him the Tenth Avenue Square wasn't going to be built if we couldn't raise $2 million in private funding for it, Mike said he and Sukey might want to help. Sukey's birthday was coming up, and he wanted to do something special for her.

A few weeks later we got the cost estimates, and it turned out the Tenth Avenue Square was actually going to cost $4 million, not $2 million. I went back to Mike to tell him. He probably thought I was just trying to get more money out of him, but $4 million was actually what it was going to cost. Mike talked to David Heller, and they decided to jointly support the Tenth Avenue Square. It was an inspiring thing for them to do. The Tenth Avenue Square is one of my favorite features on the High Line. From the start, when our design team began to define their vision for the High Line, they said they wanted to cut into the structure and reveal it from the interior rather than just build onto it. The Tenth Avenue Square shows that idea in an exciting way.

That night marked a turning point for the capital campaign, and for our organization. Each of the five couples who attended made a major gift in the weeks that followed.

JOSH

The planning team at Hudson Yards Development Corporation presented diagrams showing that you'd need to remove the supports for the High Line in order to build an underground parking garage on the eastern yards. They wanted to tear down the High Line to build a parking garage! They said they could build something new in the High Line's place that would be a lot like the High Line—an elevated park on top of new retail stores. We nicknamed this idea the Faux Line.

It was time to get people riled up. We designed postcards and flyers to mail out to our entire list, asking everybody to send letters and e-mails to the MTA in support of keeping the High Line at the rail yards. We shot a video of Edward Norton to go along with the postcards. In the video, Edward points down at the High Line from a rooftop above the rail yards. He says, "This is what they want to tear down. What do they want to tear it down for? They want to build a parking garage. A parking garage!" He talks about the plans to build a new, replacement High Line and refers to it by our nickname, the Faux Line. He says, "They tell us it'll be better than the old High Line. They said the same thing when they tore down Penn Station in 1963. Have you been to Penn Station lately?" We had prodded Edward to sound very indignant about it all, and the result was a strong, almost inflammatory video. We planned to post it on YouTube and thought it would create quite a sensation.

ROBERT

As a result of some of our outreach on the rail yards, Congressman Nadler sent a letter to the governor stating his support of retaining the High Line. A copy of the letter must have gone to Dan Doctoroff, because when Phil and I went into a meeting with Dan shortly after that, he was concerned about the letter. He impressed upon us how important the rail yards project was to the City and that things needed to go forward smoothly.

We felt we needed to fight for the High Line at the rail yards, and we knew our supporters cared about it and were looking to us to guide them. But at the same time, the City was our partner. The High Line would not have been under construction if it hadn't been for the Bloomberg administration and, in particular, Dan's team. Dan told us that he did not want to tear down the High Line at the rail yards. He said, "If the cost is not prohibitive, we will keep it." Meanwhile, Douglas Durst, who was partnering with Vornado, had leaked a study saying it would cost $110 million to keep the High Line on the rail yards site.

It was a tough decision for us, but we decided not to release the postcard campaign. We had boxes and boxes of postcards we had to recycle. We also never posted the Edward Norton video.

We worried that we might one day regret holding fire. But shortly after that, we won our first small victory on the rail yards. In the RFP issued to developers, the MTA said they would prefer to keep the High Line at the rail yards, although they remained concerned about cost and feasibility. They asked developers to submit two sets of financial estimates that showed options with and without the High Line. Our fear was that the developers would pad the estimates for keeping the High Line. But the design guidelines in the RFP included some important requirements that were very helpful to us. We'd made a few small, important wins.

Those first small wins, and other larger ones that have come since then, were due largely to Amanda Burden's pushing very strongly for us, Christine Quinn's pushing for us, and to Dan Doctoroff, who, one step at a time, integrated the High Line into the rail yards planning process. We also had fantastic support from the community, notably from the coalition called Hudson Yards Community Advisory Committee, led by Anna Levin, from Community Board 4. HYCAC made saving the High Line at the rail yards one of its top priorities, alongside affordable housing. Our board felt passionate about it, too, as did our staff, Peter Mullan especially. They put more spit and vinegar into it than Josh and I did. It takes a lot of energy and time to fight these battles, and Josh and I sometimes grew weary of the fight.

JOSH

Tiffany & Co. was opening a new store on Wall Street, and in conjunction with the opening, the Tiffany & Co. Foundation wanted to make three major gifts to different parks in Lower Manhattan. Diane Nixa and Robert went up to Fernanda Kellogg and Anisa Kamadoli Costa at the foundation to propose that the High Line be one of the recipients. Diane thought the meeting went well. Fernanda called a few weeks later, and as the call flashed on hold, Diane told everyone in the office, "If I give you the signal, cheer so that Fernanda can hear you." As she spoke to Fernanda, Diane started smiling. She made a rolling motion with her hand, and we all cheered loudly. The Tiffany & Co. Foundation was making a $1 million gift. It was our first gift from a corporate foundation. We hoped it would inspire other companies to support the project in a similar way.

ROBERT

A writer named Adam Sternbergh called us from *New York* magazine. His editors wanted to do a High Line story.

Josh and I could tell during the interviews that Adam was going to focus on real estate and the High Line. There had been a lot of attention on new developments as construction on the park advanced. Developers were bringing prominent architects to the neighborhood. Joe Rose, who had once been opposed to the High Line, was the developer of Barry Diller's IAC building; by building Frank Gehry's first major building in New York City, he helped define the High Line neighborhood as one of architectural innovation. Alf Naman had followed, with HL23, a condominium designed by Neil Denari, and 100 Eleventh Avenue, designed by Jean Nouvel. André Balazs was building the Standard Hotel, designed by Todd Schliemann at Polshek Partnership—the building would bridge over the High Line. Some people thought the High Line was responsible for all the activity, but a real estate boom was happening all over the city. The architecture around the High Line was interesting, though, and there were famous people involved, so we got more attention.

New York magazine ended up putting the story on the cover. The illustration showed the words *High Line* spelled out in big letters made out of skyscrapers. The tagline was "How a Park Built on a Junk Heap Became a Glamorous Symbol of Everything You Love and Hate About the New New York."

JOSH

The article was kind to Robert and me personally, but it essentially said that luxury real estate and high-end retail were going ruin the High Line and turn it into a symbol for the crass materialism of New York City at that particular moment in history. We were saddened and worried that the writer's perspective might reflect a broader perception. I'd had some of my own concerns about the forces we'd tapped into to drive the project forward. But I held on to the hope that it would all create something good in the end.

When you read the piece now, you see how much it reflects the moment at which it was written. In May 2007, the real estate bubble was huge.

ROBERT

We started doing pizza parties at the Fulton and Chelsea-Elliott houses, and we got to know many more residents in these two complexes than we had when we invited them to design briefings by architects.

The pizza parties became even more successful when we added photography to the mix. We hired a photographer named Tom Kletecka. I'd seen him working at the Marc Jacobs store in the West Village during the holidays. He had a backdrop with a Santa on it, and you could stand in front it and have your photo taken with Santa—it was a trendier version of the kind of backdrop photography used to do student portraits in grade schools, or at Sears.

At first we brought Tom into our benefit events, to have our guests pose in front of a High Line backdrop. The backdrop was made from a Joel Sternfeld photo taken at the rail yards, and when you stood in front of it, it really looked like you were on the High Line.

When we saw how much people loved doing this, we expanded it into something we called the High Line Portrait

Project, which involved the whole community around the High Line. Tom set up the backdrop in venues throughout the neighborhood, and we invited people to come have their photo taken, eat some pizza, and talk about the High Line. We'd print the photo right there, and they could take it home. Because the High Line was a dream that was coming true, we also asked them to write down their dreams. We made posters with montages of the photos and put them up on construction fencing near the High Line. We put also put them online, with each person's dream listed beneath their photo. People loved it. They could visualize themselves up on the High Line and started asking when it was going to open, what were the access points, what kinds of things would be up there.

JOSH

In October 2007 we finally had a chance to give our supporters a look at the rail yards section. The City and CSX agreed to let us bring people up there during Open House New York weekend.

We planned for months in advance. We were in the early stages of negotiating with the City to be the conservancy that one day would run the public park on the High Line, and we had to prove that we could handle large crowds safely.

We had tour slots for seven hundred people. We posted them on an online reservation system, and within five minutes of our opening the system, all the slots were taken. The phones immediately started ringing. People were very upset that they couldn't get a slot. Some of them yelled at Meredith Taylor, the staff member coordinating the event. Some of them cried. Then Meredith started crying, because so many people were yelling at her.

That weekend, virtually every single member of our staff and all our active volunteers were on the High Line to manage the tours. It was a crisp October day, and the tall, wheat-colored grasses looked just like they did in the autumn photos Joel Sternfeld had taken there years before. The people who came were thrilled finally to be able to set foot on the High Line. Many had been following the project for years. It made us understand the pent-up demand that had been created by eight years of media attention and no public access.

ROBERT

Five developers submitted proposals for the rail yards in response to the RFP. Three of them—Brookfield Properties, Extell Development, and The Related Companies—showed plans with the entire High Line preserved at the site. Tishman Speyer showed plans with a little of the High Line torn down, and the Durst Organization/Vornado Realty Trust showed a lot torn down.

The MTA exhibited all five proposals at a storefront near Grand Central Terminal. Steven Holl had designed Extell's proposal. It was the most creative and the most beautiful. Holl had eliminated the need to build an expensive platform over the yards by putting all the buildings around the perimeter and suspending a green park from cables over the tracks. You could tell immediately it wouldn't be seriously considered by HYDC and the MTA because it was so different from the vision they'd outlined in their guidelines.

The worst proposal for the High Line was the Durst/Vornado plan. In our meetings with him and in the press, Douglas Durst had made no secret that that he didn't like the High Line. We knew that if Durst/Vornado were selected, we'd be in for a battle.

Standing by the Durst/Vornado model, I started to talk to the woman next to me about how terrible it was. It showed almost all of the High Line gone, replaced by a glassed-in galleria called the Skyline—they said it was going to be a twenty-first-century version of the High Line. The woman tried to tell me how the proposal actually made sense, and I started arguing with her. I had already raised my voice when I recognized her. I was yelling at Helena Durst, the daughter of Douglas Durst.

Even during our worst battles, Josh and I have always tried to be friendly with the people who've opposed us. I went to find Josh and asked him to go over and talk to Helena Durst and to please be nice to her.

Why Should They Turn It Over to Us?

JOSH

When it came time for us to maintain the park on the High Line, we would need to be able to raise the funds. Diane Nixa made us switch to professional fund-raising software, Raiser's Edge, which Juliet had tried to persuade us to do for years. She hired an events manager, Tara Morris, and a new assistant, Sanaya Kaufman, who ended up running our new membership program. Diane convinced us that we had to expand our pool of donors, so we brought in a direct-mail consultant, developed letters, bought mailing lists, and started to send out membership solicitations.

I was a person who threw out, unopened, virtually every piece of direct mail I received. Direct-mail-speak is very different from the language we had been using with supporters. When our mailings started to look like junk mail to me, I raised all sorts of objections. Our consultant kept telling me, "You are not the audience." Robert and I developed such a tense relationship with the consultant that we felt it best not to renew our contract with her, even though she'd launched a program for us that performed incredibly well.

Almost a year to the day after Diane Nixa had started working for the High Line, the New York City Ballet hired her away from us. In part, she was lured by a prestigious job at a more established organization, but she had also been unhappy at the High Line. Everything had been a fire drill with us, and Robert and I had stuck our noses in everything and challenged many of her recommendations. Before she left, she sat us down and explained the things that had gone wrong. It was a hard talk for Robert and me to sit through, but we learned from it. Later we hired a workplace coach named Sarah Holland to help us address some of the issues Diane had raised.

Soon after Diane's departure, we moved our office. We got priced out of the Meatpacking District—rents were still rising across the city. We found a bigger space at a better price on the eighth floor of a gallery building on West Twentieth Street. From the windows you could see new buildings that were popping up around the High Line, designed by Frank Gehry, Shigeru Ban, Annabelle Selldorf, Gary Handel, and Jean Nouvel. Across the street was a medium-security women's prison in an Art Deco building that dated to the 1930s, like the High Line. The exercise yard was on the roof. If you stood by our windows at around 3:00 p.m., the inmates, getting their afternoon break, would wave and hoot at you from inside their fenced-in pen.

ROBERT

We were following the path of Central Park Conservancy and other conservancies, which meant we had to negotiate an agreement with the City. This would require us to raise the money each year to maintain the park, and at the same time it would give us the power to run the park ourselves under the jurisdiction of the Parks Department. At first there was some reluctance from the City, because we had no track record running parks. Sections one and two of the High Line were going to cost more than $150 million to build, and more than $100 million of that was coming from the City. Why should they turn it over to us? Other conservancies had started more slowly, supplementing the Parks Department's efforts, and they built over time to the point where they took over running the park entirely. We were suggesting that we should run it from day one. It wasn't clear what the alternative might be. The City wasn't saying that they could increase the Parks Department's budget to allow it to maintain the High Line.

John Alschuler suggested that we bring in Rich Davis to help us. Rich was an attorney who headed the board of another park conservancy, the Randall's Island Sports Foundation, which had negotiated its own license agreement. Rich's advice and advocacy with the Parks Department jump-started the process. A challenge gift from Donald Pels and Wendy Keys also helped. Don and Wendy wanted to let the City know that the only way that funders would continue to support Friends of the High Line was if we ran the park. To meet Don and Wendy's challenge, we had to complete the license agreement and match their $3 million pledge with $3 million in new gifts.

Staffing for the park was our other need. Our original plan was to hire two heads, one for horticulture and one for operations. I had no expertise in these areas, so I asked Patrick Cullina, head of horticulture at the Brooklyn Botanic Garden, to help us interview candidates. Pat had been part of a committee that the City put together to review the plant species that had been selected for the High Line by Piet Oudolf and James Corner Field Operations, and I was impressed by his appreciation for the High Line and for Piet Oudolf's vision. Pat questioned the idea of having separate heads of horticulture and operations. On the High Line, he argued, these two jobs would be so closely related that it was a mistake to think of them separately.

During the interview process, I had my George Bush moment—I call it that, although I was no fan of George Bush. When he was running for president, Bush brought Dick Cheney in to help him find a vice-presidential candidate, and he ended up picking Cheney himself. We had brought in Pat Cullina to help us find someone to run the park, and I started to think Pat Cullina himself would be the perfect person for the job. I didn't know if we could get him. At the time, he had one of the best horticulture jobs in New York City. But I raised the subject with him, and he said he was interested.

At the same time that Pat Cullina was deliberating, we hired Melissa Fisher, who'd formerly worked at the Horticultural Society of New York. My thought was that someone more senior, perhaps Pat, would later be hired above her. Melissa was smart, with an eager attitude toward tackling the many unknowns we'd face in caring for gardens on a bridge structure thirty feet in the air. Her immediate job was to develop a horticultural maintenance program and to oversee the planting process—the contractors started to install the grasses and perennials in the spring of 2008, and we needed someone to monitor their work. She was young, but I felt that she could grow in the job and perhaps one day run the whole park by herself.

JOSH

When visitors came to the construction site, we made them sign waivers and wear hard hats. The contractors' stairs were steep and scary and smelled of pee. Once you were up on the High Line, you had to step on and off concrete ledges at different levels, taking care not to trip on electrical conduits and water pipes. It was an exciting site to visit.

A cement planking system like ours had never been built before. As the planks of different forms and sizes were lifted into place, you could see the pathways of the High Line taking shape. The landscape contractors came in next, to lay down layers of gravel and netting for drainage, followed by the soil and plants. Even for people who were familiar with building sites, it was unusual.

Lisa Falcone came to visit the site in March 2008. She'd never been up on the High Line before, even though she and Philip had already made a very generous gift to help us build the stairs at Fourteenth Street. It was a gray day, and there were patches of snow and ice on the walkways. Lisa had recently cut her long black hair in a flattering bob, and she was wearing fabulous silver sneakers that laced halfway to her knees—I'd told her assistant that the high stiletto heels I'd seen Lisa wear in the past wouldn't work on the icy construction site.

It was the first time I'd spent any time alone with Lisa. She didn't say much at first. She just walked along, looking around, taking it all in. I had the impression she was underwhelmed.

About halfway through our walk, she started talking, slowly at first. She said she lived close to Central Park, and she'd often thought about the people who'd built it, and what a great thing they had done for the city, so many years ago. Someday, she said, New Yorkers would look back in a similar way at the people who'd made the High Line. It was part of history. How many people get to make a park in New York City? She'd been talking about it with her young daughters, telling them how amazing it was to be able to build a park. I'd said similar things in the past, but Lisa felt it very strongly—there was a tremor in her voice—and she made me believe in these ideas with a new kind of conviction.

ROBERT

In March 2008, Tishman Speyer won the bid to develop the rail yards, but six weeks later, the deal fell apart. The housing bubble was starting to burst, and financing for large real estate projects like the rail yards was drying up. Related stepped in, made a new deal with the MTA, and became the developer for the rail yards. We were excited by the rapid and surprising turn of events. While Tishman Speyer's proposal had shown a small part of the High Line torn down, Rob Speyer had been an early supporter of our efforts, and we were optimistic we could work with him to resolve the rail yards issue. Related's proposal, however, had shown the entire High Line preserved. And Vishaan Chakrabarti worked at Related. We knew Vishaan well from his time at City Planning, when he'd overseen the West Chelsea rezoning, under Amanda Burden.

Unfortunately, we started to hear that Related had some concerns about the High Line, too. They were especially concerned about the spur over Tenth Avenue. They told us that the darkness it cast on the street would make it hard to market a commercial office tower at the corner of Tenth Avenue and Thirtieth Street, and that it was unlikely that they could keep that portion of the High Line.

JOSH

Defaults on subprime mortgages were in the news, but for many of us in New York City, they remained abstract, something that was happening in Florida and Las Vegas. In New York, the money was still pumping. We raised $2.5 million at our summer benefit that year—the most we'd ever raised at an event—and our membership mailings were performing well. We built strong relationships with new donors and planned to do a round of major solicitations. It would be the next surge in our $50 million capital campaign. We'd raised about $23 million to date.

New York was also still home to big, splashy events, and now we were going to have one of them on the High Line. Calvin Klein Collection was celebrating its fortieth anniversary during Fashion Week. Malcolm Carfrae, who headed communications for the company, wanted the celebration to act as a gift to the city. He had arranged for the company to make a major contribution to help us meet maintenance costs for the High Line when it opened, and that helped us get the party approved by the City.

John Pawson, the minimalist architect who had designed the Calvin Klein stores, designed the event structure. A basic party tent was at its core, but the interior and exterior were fitted out at a level of detail and expense that made it look as if a sleek, marble-clad museum had risen from this unlikely corner of Tenth Avenue and Thirtieth Street, near the entrance to the Lincoln Tunnel. Inside, there was a light installation by the artist James Turrell and a series of tiered levels stepping upward to the High Line, at the curve between Twenty-ninth and Thirtieth streets.

This part of the High Line was still bare concrete, cleared of gravel and ballast. The event team dressed it with grasses, perennials, and thousands of long-stemmed white roses—their interpretation of what the High Line would one day become.

The party was on a warm summer night right after Labor Day—the first big event of Fashion Week. Black cars lined up along Tenth Avenue. Each time someone stepped onto the red carpet—Halle Berry, Brooke Shields, Naomi Watts, Anna Wintour—hundreds of flashes fired off. The High Line was packed with magazine editors, designers, stylists, models, and actors. The scent of roses hung thick in the air. The party had the kind of exuberance that makes you feel that New York City is the only place in the world.

A week later, Lehman Brothers collapsed.

We had a High Line event scheduled for that night. Tom Colicchio hosted a fund-raiser at Craftsteak, his restaurant at the corner of Fifteenth Street and Tenth Avenue, now called Colicchio and Sons. We'd done a similar event the previous year, called the High Line Chefs Dinner, and our supporters remembered it fondly. At this year's Chefs Dinner, however, many seats remained empty, because the people who'd purchased them had been called to their offices to manage fallout from what would soon be known as the biggest bankruptcy in American history. Marooned spouses thumbed nervously at their BlackBerrys, and by the time dessert landed, entire tables had decamped. The next morning, the Dow dropped five hundred points.

We were just months away from opening the first section of the High Line. The license agreement we were negotiating with the City would require us to pay for virtually all its maintenance and operations with funds we raised from charitable contributions—more than $2 million every year. Besides the maintenance obligation, we still had more than $25 million left to raise in our capital campaign. And the economy was plummeting.

All the major solicitations we were planning got shelved. Robert and I phoned around for advice. Some people told us to pull the plug on the capital campaign—that it would be years before we saw another big gift. Others, people who had worked in fund-raising during previous crashes, told us to keep going— reduce your expectations, be willing to wait longer for gifts, use the tough times as a reason to talk frankly with donors. But if you stop the campaign, they told us, you are doomed.

It was hard to book meetings. People didn't want to see us. When we did get a meeting, people said, "Not now. We can't consider it now." To keep our top supporters in the loop, every few weeks I would send an e-mail with a picture that showed the progress on the High Line. I sent one of these out around Thanksgiving, with a short note about all the things we were grateful for. After all, even in these bad times, there was much to be thankful for at the High Line.

Barry Diller responded to one of those e-mails. He said, "I'm concerned about the economy and its effect on the High Line. We should talk." Robert and I made an appointment to see him. We brought all our budgets, our revenue history, and our projections for how much the High Line was going to cost to build and operate. We'd prepared carefully, because we expected that he would ask difficult questions. We told him that section one was now paid for, but that we needed to raise more capital funds for section two, to ensure that all the best design features, like the Flyover and the Thirtieth Street Cut-out, weren't cut from the scope, and that we also aimed to raise funds for an endowment, to lay the foundation for long-term financial sustainability. We explained how hard it was for the two of us to raise funds in an environment like this, because we didn't have the capacity to set an example with a major gift of our own, but Barry, as a leading supporter, could have a different kind of influence. If he and Diane invited people to a celebratory event at the opening of the High Line, they could talk about the need to support this exciting City project. We suggested that a challenge gift might jump-start fund-raising. Robert and I had agreed that I would say the number—ten million dollars—but it caught in my throat like a small, dry feather; it actually made me cough. So Robert jumped in and he said it. Barry wrote the number down on a piece of paper and said he'd discuss it with the family. After the meeting, we did our best to put it out of our minds. A few weeks later, after lunch, in the queue of waiting e-mails was one from Barry Diller, just a single sentence telling me that the family had decided to make a $10 million challenge gift.

From the time we started working on the High Line, people stepped up to support it in surprising and extraordinary ways. This one topped them all. The funds were badly needed, but behind the stunning number was something even bigger, a belief in the High Line and in what it could mean. Many times, that day and in the weeks that followed, Robert and I tried to craft the words to thank Barry, Diane, Alex, and Tatiana, but we could never really convey the depth of what we felt.

ROBERT

Phil Aarons likes getting things off the ground. He was our board chair from the beginning—he played the part even before we officially made him our board chair. As we started becoming more successful, I knew that Phil would eventually want to step down.

Who would be the next board chair? My first thought was to get someone who would help us with fund-raising. Phil never liked to ask for money. Josh and I were doing every ask. It would be great to have a board chair who was giving a lot of money, to the High Line and to other causes, doing those asks. But we also still faced a lot of complex logistical challenges, and because of those challenges, I talked to Phil almost every day—about elements of the design, our relationship with the City, the construction process, the rail yards fight. So the chair's job wasn't just about fund-raising. We needed a hands-on chair who would be willing to talk to me day after day. I started thinking about John Alschuler. He had played a critical role with the economic feasibility study, and he'd been overseeing all our work on the rail yards. He had the ability to frame complex ideas in simple ways. I liked working with him, and other board members respected him.

My assumption was that Phil would step down right after we opened section one of the High Line. But he called me several months before we opened and said, "I want to step down now so someone new has the opportunity to be the chair at the ribbon cutting." He thought it would elevate the new board chair to be in the leadership position when we opened. It would raise that person in the eyes of our City partners and our supporters, and give the new chair the standing to move the organization from an advocacy organization into a conservancy that could run the park. By letting someone else stand in the limelight when the park opened, Phil was doing what he'd always told us to do: giving credit to others. He always said that the more we gave other people credit for the High Line's success, the more success the High Line would have.

I was in Texas with my family when Phil called me. I'd already been thinking for over a year that John might be a good chair. I'd talked to Josh about it, and he had agreed. I called John as soon as I finished talking to Phil. He said he was flattered and honored to be asked, but that he needed a day or two to think about it.

JOSH

In May 2009, on an evening one month before we were scheduled to open section one, our board members walked the entire High Line, from Thirty-fourth Street to Gansevoort Street. It was Robert's idea. The walk would commemorate that we were finally going to open the park, and it would honor Phil and his leadership.

Many of our board members had previously visited the High Line in sections, but they had never walked the whole structure all at once. I'd done it only a few times myself. To go from one end to another felt like a true journey. In some ways it was like walking a time line of the project itself. We started at the rail yards, where the natural landscape was still in place. This was the High Line as Robert and I had originally seen it, as Joel Sternfeld had photographed it. In this section, our organization was still in advocacy mode, as we had been at the start, fighting the people who saw the High Line as a relic and an obstacle. Then we moved into the construction site for section two, which was bare concrete. Here we were looking at the High Line's transformation in its early stages, the past wiped away, awaiting the future. Then, at Twentieth Street, we passed through a gate and into section one. Here the park was almost complete. The contractors were still busily working on site, and there was still much to be done, but there was no longer any doubt that the curtain would rise and a drama would play out.

We held our board meeting at the Standard Hotel, which had opened a few months earlier, straddling the High Line between Little West Twelfth and Thirteenth streets. When Robert and I started the High Line project ten years earlier, this site had been a meatpacking plant. Now we rode up in the fashionably dark elevator, with an artist's video playing in the wall of the elevator cabin, showing souls rising from purgatory, into the heavens, and then falling back down into hell.

Sitting around the long, shiny table in the Standard's meeting room, which overlooked the High Line through plate-glass windows, we toasted our new, official partnership with the City of New York and the Parks Department. The license agreement was finished; it had taken three years to complete. When the High Line opened to the public a few weeks later, Friends of the High Line would be the first park conservancy in New York City also to be the group that had originally called for the park's creation and that was in place, operating the new park, on the day it opened.

Adrian Benepe, the parks commissioner, spoke seriously about the burden we were assuming. He knew better than any of us the challenges of running a park. This led to a discussion about possible crowding on the High Line. We had no idea how many people would come. There was no real way of predicting. But we could feel it in the air: the city was excited. Robert explained his plans for crowd control. In our opening months, two staff members with clickers would be stationed at every access point, counting the visitors. If we hit a certain number, access points would be closed until enough people had exited to safely allow people up again.

There was more emotion in the room than at our usual board meetings, because our board members had done so much to bring us to this point. We acknowledged Amanda Burden and Gifford Miller, two of the High Line's first great champions. A special note was made of Amanda's recent push for the City to certify a ULURP application for approval to acquire the rail yards section of the High Line from the railroad. The transfer of ownership itself might take years—there were still many differences of opinion between the MTA, Related, the City, and Friends of the High Line about how the High Line should be treated at the site—but it was an optimistic step forward; it indicated that the City expected that one day a transfer of ownership would occur, and that the rail yards section would become part of the park. We also thanked all the board members who'd helped carry us through this period of economic turmoil, especially Alex von Furstenberg and Wendy Keys, who'd launched and sustained our capital campaign with multiple major gifts. Several people made speeches about Phil. We toasted him and all he'd done for the High Line, and we elected John Alschuler to be our next board chair.

ROBERT

I met Phil when we were just starting the High Line, and he became my mentor. He and Shelley were now two of my closest friends.

There are so many people who helped make the High Line happen. Gifford provided political will and key public funding. Phil provided strategy and confidence, and served as a kind of moral compass. Some people think Phil was helpful because he was a developer and his standing gave us credibility. Joan Davidson, a supporter of parks and historic preservation in New York City, asked Phil at an early event if he was the first "adult" to get behind the High Line. But Phil also had a strong sense of what made the High Line important and interesting. He loved the odd and unlikely parts of the project, such as the ideas competition, which had made sense for us as an organization, because that sort of openness to creative ideas is what we stood for. If there was a choice between doing something safe and easy and doing something more promising but risky, Phil always encouraged us to take the risk.

Cutting the Ribbon

JOSH

On June 1, one week before the High Line opened to the public, Barry Diller and Diane von Furstenberg hosted a preview dinner on the High Line. Two hundred guests arrived in early evening and walked up the Gansevoort Stairs, setting foot in the park for the first time. Some were our board members and top donors. Others were friends whom Barry and Diane had invited, people who might be interested in supporting the project. Only a few days of construction work remained, and we strode along the walkways, where the grasses pushed up between the tapering concrete planks, just as they had in the designers' plans. We passed under the Standard Hotel and through the Fourteenth Street passage to the Sundeck, where a bar was set for cocktails. When the sun began to drop behind the river, we moved on to dinner at two long tables that ran the length of the Chelsea Market Passage.

We'd been planning this dinner for months. It was here that we would announce the Diller–von Furstenberg family's challenge. Robin Pogrebin, a reporter from the *Times*, had been quietly briefed. She was sitting at one of the long tables and would run an article the following morning.

It began just as we'd planned it. The rhythm of my remarks built up, and when I announced the family's challenge, the applause and cheering were thunderous. Then I went into the next part—how we should be motivated by Diane and Barry's leadership to meet their challenge, so that we could complete section two of the High Line and create an endowment for the future. It was then that Lisa Falcone walked toward me and asked for the microphone. I hesitated; this wasn't part of the script. Lisa whispered in my ear, gave me a kind of hug, and the microphone passed from my hand to hers. When she announced that she and her husband, Philip, were so inspired by Barry and Diane that they would match the $10 million challenge with a $10 million gift of their own, there was an instant of stunned silence, followed by even more thunderous applause.

As much as reporters and gossips tried to capture that moment, nobody got it quite right. Lisa and I had met many times during that terrible year of the crash. Each time we met, I'd tell her how the project was progressing and lay out our needs for the future, asking if she and Philip could help us. I didn't explicitly beg, but the year had been a trying one, and I think she could read a kind of pleading in my eyes. She would look at the materials I put in front of her, touch her throat, and say, "This is so beautiful," shaking her head with regret. I knew she wanted to do something, that she couldn't do it right then, but that when the moment was right, she would. She was one of the few people I'd told about Diane and Barry's challenge. She also knew my birthday was coming up. That night, Stephen had mentioned it to her casually during cocktails, right before dinner, out on the Sundeck. The dinner was on June 1; my birthday is June 3. After she took the microphone from my hand, and just before she made her wonderful surprise announcement, Lisa had wrapped her long, smooth arm around my neck, pulled my head close, and whispered in my ear, "Happy birthday."

ROBERT

It was a race at the end to get everything ready for the ribbon cutting. Even just two days before, a lot of work was still taking place. But we had set a date with the mayor, and so we had to finish.

During the early stages of the design process, I'd often worried that the park we were planning wouldn't live up to the original landscape in Joel Sternfeld's photos. As we neared completion, a different worry set in: we'd received so much good press that I feared the final outcome wouldn't live up to the hype.

I worried about the plantings most of all. Even under the best conditions, we didn't know how well anything on the High Line would grow. Would the drainage system actually work? If it didn't, the roots would all rot. The High Line is basically a bridge, with air flowing over and under it, so it freezes quickly in winter and cooks in the summer. I was convinced that with temperatures going up and down, everything was going to die.

I asked Piet Oudolf about it. Piet, a renowned Dutch planting designer, had selected and sited all the plants in partnership with the landscape architects at James Corner Field Operations. He said not to worry; it would be fine. Just as he'd told me, the spring bulbs started coming up, and the plants started flowering, some as early as March, while there was still snow on the ground. No one was up on the High Line except for our staff and the contractors. Just our small lucky group got to enjoy the flowers from the forty thousand bulbs the Dutch Bulb Association had donated. By the time of the ribbon cutting, the plants had filled in nicely. People couldn't believe that they had been planted for so short a time.

Our staff organized a small event up on the High Line for the night before the ribbon cutting. Someone had given us a magnum of champagne, and we opened that, and everyone smiled through their exhaustion. By this point we'd all been working seven days a week for quite a while.

I was confident. Patrick Cullina had come on board to oversee all the park's operations and horticulture for our first year. He and Melissa Fisher hired a terrific group of gardeners and custodians, and we had faith in their ability to run the High Line well, even though no one had any real idea of what it was going to be like to manage a park thirty feet in the air.

I'd often wondered if I'd be able to enjoy the success of the High Line. I've always had a better time with problems. But from the night of Diane and Barry's dinner, I was able to enjoy it.

People were coming up to me and saying, "It's amazing, congratulations," and I allowed myself to feel that we actually had done something special. James LaForce, who had helped us with our very first fund-raiser, sent an e-mail saying, "Now you don't have to do anything else in your life, you can quit." It made me feel less embarrassed about all the self-help books I'd read over the years.

JOSH

The ribbon cutting took place under the Standard Hotel. We chose the space because the walkway there was big enough for a few rows of seats, and it was a photogenic spot, where we could put the podium in front of the expanse of grasses and trees.

We all took our turns at the podium: Mayor Bloomberg, Congressman Nadler, Speaker Quinn, Borough President Stringer, Amanda Burden, Adrian Benepe, Diane, Barry, the Falcones, Robert, and me. By then, I'd stood in front of a lot of microphones and talked to a lot of audiences, but I'd never faced a group of people as joyful as the people who were there that day. I couldn't really look at Stephen or my family or our staff, because some of them were crying, and I knew that if I looked at them, I would cry, too. My glance kept coming back to

Patti Harris, Mayor Bloomberg's first deputy mayor. During the seven years we'd been working with the City, her name had been endlessly invoked: "Amanda (or Adrian or Dan) will take it up to Patti." To look at her from the lectern and see her smiling made me appreciate just how many different people had come together around the project.

ROBERT

My parents had flown in from Texas for the opening, just as they had for so many other important milestones in the High Line project over the years. My mother has never missed one of our benefits.

So much about the High Line reminded me of my mother, especially in the early days, when it seemed like such an unusual idea. She had taught me to find the beauty in the unexpected and the odd, things that other people might not notice, and to pursue my passions even if they were unconventional.

My father was more conventional, and it took me a few years to realize how he had influenced my involvement in the High Line, too. He was in the wholesale jewelry business, but he spent all his free time working with nonprofit organizations, and he had a passion for architecture, preservation, and parks.

By the time we opened the High Line, I had spent ten years working on a project that combined so many aspects of both my parents.

JOSH

There were too many hands with too many scissors, and assembling the group for the cameras was done in a breathless rush, and then, snip, after all those speeches and all those years of work, it was over.

We hadn't publicized the ribbon cutting, but people on the streets below had heard the speeches and gone to the stairs to wait. The word had also traveled quickly online—*the High Line is opening, right now!*—and people who'd been following the project for years rushed over to be the first to visit the park.

I didn't see people come up the stairs. It was more like an instant transformation, as if Samantha from *Bewitched* had wrinkled up her nose, and bing, the High Line was full of people looking down from the railings, trying out the benches, sipping coffee from paper cups, taking photographs of one another. Among them were a bride and groom in full wedding regalia. They'd heard about the ribbon cutting on the radio, thrown on their tux and gown, and run over to do their photos.

It was disorienting to see so many strangers on the High Line. For so long it had been ours alone.

At the staff toast on the High Line the night before, I had marveled at the park in its empty, just-completed state. Architects said it looked exactly like the renderings—which almost never happens, because renderings tend to present idealized visions that cannot always be achieved. But in this case the idealized vision had been achieved. Our crew had been over every inch of the High Line with tweezers and polish. The glass and steel sparkled, and the planting beds were fluffed to look impeccably wild. After ten years of work, I found it hard to imagine that anything could be more beautiful than the empty, pristine High Line that night before we opened—it was a perfect thing.

With all the different people who poured into the park on the morning of the ribbon cutting, the High Line became a little less perfect and a lot more beautiful. It wasn't just ours any longer, and it had come to life.

AFTERWORD

ROBERT

We cut the ribbon on section one on June 8, 2009. During the two years that followed, more than four million people visited. About half were from New York and half were out-of-town visitors, split between the United States and other countries. This popularity was far beyond anything Josh and I had ever hoped for or expected. We never really knew how many people would come, but we were guessing about 300,000 per year. We thought the numbers might drop over time, but they have grown. On a single recent weekend in June, more than 100,000 people visited.

JOSH

The crowds during the busiest hours—on sunny Saturdays and Sundays, between noon and six p.m.—freaked me out at first. Everywhere I looked, I imagined an accident about to happen. But the accidents didn't happen. People had their picnics, walked hand in hand, read their books, talked to the gardeners, ate their popsicles, looked at the public artworks we'd installed, and dozed on the lounges at the Diller–von Furstenberg Sundeck.

If you go early enough, around eight a.m., you'll have the High Line pretty much all to yourself. The gardeners are just starting their weeding, watering, and pruning—it's one of the few times they can work steadily without stopping to answer questions from visitors about whatever it is they're planting or pruning.

Before and after sunset, there's a more social mood. People slow down, walking the pathways, leisurely and aimlessly. As the sky dims from orange to inky blue, the High Line's planting beds begin to glow, lit from within. Virtually all the High Line's lighting fixtures are concealed in stainless-steel handrails, positioned at waist level or below, nestled behind grasses. Hervé Descottes, at L'Observatoire International, designed the system so that light would not shine in your eyes and you would be better able to appreciate the night sky.

You see a lot of people holding hands on the High Line. In general you don't see a lot of people holding hands in New York City—it's not a hand-holding kind of city—but you see it on the High Line.

In Italy there's a traditional walk called the *passeggiata*. In small towns and big cities, people come out in the early evening to do a leisurely, theatrical promenade through one of the main streets or a central piazza.

When we started working on the High Line, I held in the back of my mind an image of the High Line as a place where something like the Italian *passeggiata* could happen—a place where people would come to stroll just for the sake of strolling, to be among their fellow citizens, to smile and flirt, to check out one another's outfits, to walk with parents after an early dinner, or to meet up for a date.

We have a great calendar of public programs, more than three hundred each year, overseen by Danya Sherman, one of the staff members at Friends of the High Line who started as an office assistant and rose to head a department. But many of my favorite happenings on the High Line are spontaneous—the things we didn't plan.

A woman named Patty Heffley lived right next to the High Line at West Twentieth Street. She'd lived there for more than thirty years. When we first opened the High Line, the security lights from a staircase shined directly into her window. At first she complained, until she discovered that the beam made her fire escape into a stage, and that there was a guaranteed audience walking past on the High Line. She started to invite singers to perform up there—she called these performances the High Line Renegade Cabaret. Word spread, crowds began gathering, and when a reporter from *The New York Times* wrote about it, it became one of the early legends of the High Line. Sadly, she had to stop doing it. Her landlord hassled her, said that it was illegal to use the fire escape that way.

Another thing you hear a lot about but don't actually see very much is sex in the windows at the Standard. As the hotel was being built, we grew aware of its theatrical relation to the High Line below, with its towering wall of bedroom windows facing directly down onto the park. We were surprised that no one commented on it until shortly after section one opened. I think nymag.com posted the first story, but it wasn't until the *New York Post* picked it up, dubbing the Standard the "Eyeful Tower," running photos of naked men and women in the windows, that the story went viral, traveling faster and farther online than any story about the High Line ever had. For months after that, you'd see crowds clustered under the Standard, looking up, waiting for something to happen, but it rarely did.

JOSH

Each time I go up the stairs, or ride up in one of elevators, I think how amazing it is that anyone can go up to the High Line anytime they want, from seven in the morning until we close. I think of all those CSX tours with Laurie Izes, the appointments and reconfirmations, making sure everyone was wearing flat shoes, signing the waivers, crawling on our bellies under the fence through the gravel and broken glass. Just the fact that people can come up here whenever they want—it's what we wanted at the start, before we began worrying about fund-raising or design choices or what size font to use in our party invitations.

Few people who come to the High Line know what it took to make it possible. I'm glad that they don't. It's a little like being the host of a party. You just want people to have a good time.

ROBERT

Many big public projects come from the top down. An elected official champions it, and it gets done. We couldn't have done the High Line without New York's elected officials, but I always describe the High Line as a bottom-up project. Josh laughs when I say it, because it sounds sort of gay, but the fact is, our project began at the community level.

I was recently on a panel with Malcolm Gladwell and I made this point, and Malcolm called me on it by saying, "It was 'bottom-up' from a bunch of very sophisticated architects and planners. I mean, if that's 'bottom-up,' I'd love to be on the bottom."

JOSH

New York is constantly changing, and the changes we've seen around the High Line will be dwarfed by the changes to come. New buildings will continue to be built around the High Line. The Whitney will open at Gansevoort Street. The rail yards development, called Hudson Yards, with twelve million square feet of new construction, will be a city unto itself, with offices, apartments, shops, a hotel, a cultural center, a park, all inhabited by millions of residents, workers, and visitors, directly next to the High Line.

People sometimes share worries with us—will this new building or that new building ruin the High Line, or will tourists ruin the High Line, or will it ruin the High Line if someone comes along after us and makes changes to the design? Robert and I are protective of the High Line, but we're also reassured by its resiliency. It's big, and it was built to carry fully loaded freight trains. We think it can hold its own against most things that happen around it.

The other day, walking to work on the High Line, I felt like I was in some kind of Dr. Suess garden as I went past the foxtail lilies, with their tall yellow plumes; the serviceberry trees, full of edible berries; and the smoke bushes, with their feathery puffs tossing in the wind. I know the names of these particular plants, but I don't know the names of most of the plants. It's not about the individual plants—it's the overall effect. Some people think of parks as being an escape from the city, but the High Line works because it never takes you away from New York. You are not in a botanical garden. You can hear horns honking. You can see traffic and taxis. It's knitted into the city. And you're not alone. You're walking up there with other New Yorkers.

In the years I've lived in New York City I've seen many landmarks vanish. Not necessarily historic or architectural landmarks, but landmarks of city life. It might be an individual business, like the Palladium, Restaurant Florent, Gotham Book Mart, or the nameless donut shop favored by drifters at the corner of West Twenty-third Street and Eighth Avenue. Or it might be an entire neighborhood, like the old Times Square, with its Howard Johnson's, China Bowl, and Gaiety male burlesque.

I've also seen an unbelievable amount of new construction: Battery Park City, Riverside South, the Hearst building, Trump Tower, and the Time Warner Center, just to begin. When I stand on the High Line at West Thirtieth Street and look toward Midtown, I don't have enough fingers to count the skyscrapers that have gone up just since Robert and I started working on this project.

In a place that changes so much, things that survive have the power to transport you. I felt it the other day as I showed a new friend around the High Line, explaining that before this neighborhood was defined by contemporary art, Google, and Martha Stewart, it was all about trains, ships, and factories. We stopped just north of West Twenty-fifth Street to look between the warehouses at a pair of smokestacks that would have been active when the High Line was built. At West Sixteenth Street, we admired the rotting pilings in the Hudson River, a view framed by the former Nabisco factory and a former refrigerated warehouse. The pilings were all that was left of the piers where ocean liners used to dock.

Robert and I wanted some of the old New York Central railroad tracks to be reinstalled on the High Line, because we loved the way they looked, and because we hoped they would help visitors sense the structure's past without having to take a history lesson. You can see the tracks clearly in early spring, when the plants are just starting to bud. What we didn't anticipate was just how lushly the plants would grow by midsummer. As I write this, you can barely see those old tracks on the High Line, because the grasses and shrubs we planted have grown so thick. When I walked with my friend the other day, I had to point out where the tracks lay, hidden in the shade of the sassafras trees.

ROBERT

I have three goals for the High Line: that it will always be well loved by New Yorkers; that it will inspire others to start their own projects; and that it will get better after Josh and I leave.

The true sign of a healthy organization is that it is not dependent on its founders. That's what I want for the High Line, for it to keep growing and changing, and not for it to be dependent on Josh, me, and the core group that started it.

When I say I hope it will inspire people, I don't mean that it should inspire people to build more parks on elevated rail structures—although there are other organizations trying to do that now, in Jersey City, for example, and in Chicago and Philadelphia, among other cities, and we support them. We were inspired by others, and I hope the High Line will encourage people to pursue all sorts of crazy projects, even if they seem, as the High Line once did, the most unlikely of dreams.

PHOTOGRAPHS

DEATH AVENUE

The West Side of Manhattan was a busy industrial waterfront for nearly a century before the High Line was built. Factories and warehouses lined its avenues, while ships, trains, and trucks brought agricultural and industrial goods to its manufacturing and distribution centers.

THE CITY OF TOMORROW

The architecture and city planning of the early twentieth
century reflected an imaginative futurism dedicated to
solving the problems of traffic congestion and dangerous
conditions associated with urban crowding. The "City of
Tomorrow" movement, which often proposed separating
transportation forms onto different levels, influenced
architecture and planning of the time.

this page
Drawing by Hugh Fer-
riss, from *Architectural
Forum*, 1927

opposite page
"King's Dream of New
York," from *King's
Views of New York*, a
popular series of il-
lustrations, 1908–1909.
The series showed
the popular fascina-
tion with futuristic
solutions to urban
problems.

BUILDING THE HIGH LINE

As part of the West Side Improvement Project, an elevated
freight viaduct was built from Thirty-fifth Street to the
St. Johns Park Terminal, at Spring Street. The structure, known
as the New York Central Elevated Spur, was under construction
from 1929 to 1934. The Miller Elevated Highway, built for
automobile traffic, rose just to the west at the same time.

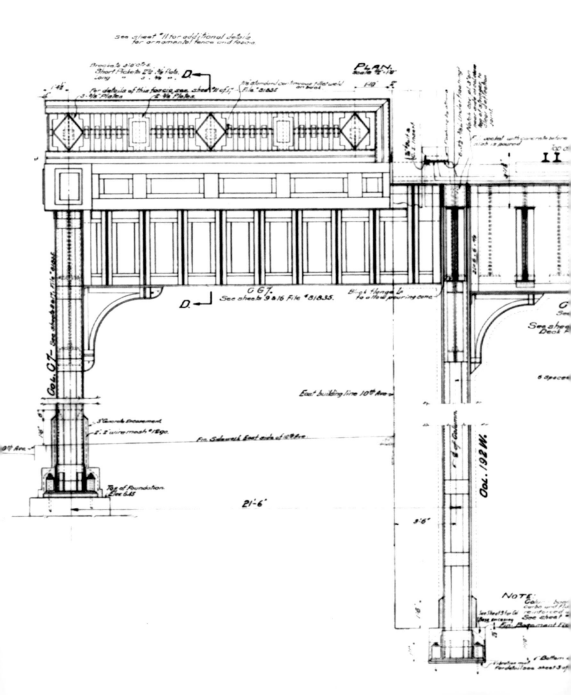

opposite page
Trains ran through the former Bell Telephone Laboratories building, now the Westbeth artist complex, on a section of the structure that was later demolished after freight traffic declined.

this page
The third-story loading dock at the Merchant's Refrigerated Warehouse on West Seventeenth Street and Tenth Avenue

AN ELEVATED RAILWAY

The High Line was built to run above private properties rather than over the avenues, and it brought trains directly through buildings at the third-story level. Many existing buildings were modified to accommodate the new elevated line, while new factories and warehouses were quickly built to take advantage of the freight delivery system it offered.

NEW YORK
CENTRAL

1559

1559

this page
A typical example of
New York Central Rail-
road's rolling stock

opposite page
A locomotive on
the High Line above
Thirtieth Street in
the 1950s

LIFELINE OF NEW YORK

From 1934 to 1980, the High Line carried meat, milk, fruit, and other agricultural goods to the refrigerated warehouses and distribution centers on the West Side. It was known as the Lifeline of New York.

Libby's —COMIN' ON THE RAILROAD

LIB-BY'S mo-vin' on the rail-road.
For a long, long stay,
That's why all us Fam-ous Foods is
So hap-py and so gay!

"YES SIR!
"We're glad that WILSON & ROGERS, Inc., have moved into St. John's Park Terminal on the NEW YORK CENTRAL'S new West Side Line. They're our commanding officers, . . . the people who will distribute us in the New York zone after Libby McNeil & Libby mobilize us in cans and bottles.
"Sure enough! We know of several other firms who have lots of freight to move that are figuring right now on getting new plants on the West Side Line, because they can save money there in several ways . . . one way is by getting just the right kind of tailor-made plants for themselves . . . And they save more by having a sidetrack right in the plant . . . for instance, after we're canned we're going to ride all the way from the cannery in a freight car right into that new warehouse . . . no traffic hazards, no extra handling for us! And we hear that some firms save enough in these ways to pay most of their rent bill . . . how's that for a saving?"

NEW YORK CENTRAL
L. C. JAMES, General Land & Tax Agent
E. D. SNOW, Industrial Agent
466 Lexington Avenue, New York City, MUrray Hill 9-8000

DISUSE

The last train ran on the High Line in 1980, reportedly pulling three carloads of frozen turkeys. With the end of train traffic, a self-seeded landscape began to grow among the gravel ballast and steel rails atop the out-of-use structure. Grasses, wildflowers, and shrubs took root and slowly took over the High Line.

EARLY EFFORTS

Peter Obletz (opposite page), a Chelsea resident, activist, and railroad enthusiast, challenged demolition efforts in the 1980s. Obletz eventually purchased the High Line from Conrail for $10, a transaction that was later overturned by the New York State Supreme Court. For a time, he lived underneath the High Line at the West Side Rail Yards, in a converted Pullman car.

In a 1981 project called "Bridge of Houses" (below), the architect Steven Holl proposed repurposing of the High Line by building housing and public space on the unused railbed.

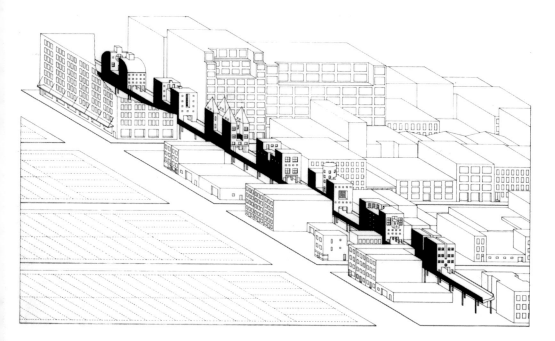

opposite page
High Line logo designed by Paula Scher in 1999

this page
Joshua David, left, and Robert Hammond, cofounders of Friends of the High Line

FRIENDS OF THE HIGH LINE

In 1999, neighborhood residents Robert Hammond and Joshua David met at a community board meeting concerning the uncertain future of the High Line. Realizing that there was no organized community movement to save the structure, they soon joined together and founded Friends of the High Line.

WALKING THE HIGH LINE, 2001–2002

Approached by Friends of the High Line, and with permission from CSX Transportation, the photographer Joel Sternfeld captured the High Line's landscape in all seasons in his book *Walking the High Line.* His evocative images built widespread public support in the community for the High Line's preservation.

HIGH LINE REAL/TY

Produced by Chelsea Property Owners, a group of concerned businesses and citizens who care about • effective, not wasteful, city spending • safety • logical economic growth for New York

WHY CAN'T JOHNNY SWING?

Because the High Line is too narrow. It won't even be able to fit this backyard playset! How useful is a park that can't even accommodate kids?

Our city needs money for important things—stop wasting money on the High Line.

Email us at highline2002@mail.com or call Doug Sarini at 212-691-5982

HIGH LINE REAL/TY

Produced by Chelsea Property Owners, a group of concerned businesses and citizens who care about • effective, not wasteful city spending • safety • logical economic growth for New York

Money doesn't grow on trees… and the last time we checked it wasn't growing in the weeds of the High Line either.

The Friends of the High Line seem to assume money for a "park in the sky" will just fall out of the sky. Their plans for funding are: "Public moneys, corporate sponsorships, foundation grants, public/private partnership and donor support." In other words, they're not sure where the money will come from. They held their big fundraiser and raised $200,000. Sounds like a lot until you realize it's less than one quarter of one percent of what even their supporters estimate the work will cost.

Perhaps The Friends of the High Line haven't heard that the City of New York is seeking money to rebuild crumbling schools, and maybe even fix the parks that we already have. Millions of dollars for a park in the sky??? Please. **New York still has not determined where it will get the $183,000,000 to finish the Hudson River Park, less than one block away!!**

2003 DESIGN IDEAS COMPETITION

In 2003, Friends of the High Line held an ideas competition.
At the time, the High Line was not yet secured for park use.
Entries did not have to be realistic or practical, but were
intended to provoke a dialogue about the High Line's future.
The open call resulted in 720 entries from thirty-six countries.

2004 DESIGN COMPETITION

In 2004, following the design ideas competition, Friends of the High Line and the City of New York released a Request For Qualifications seeking interdisciplinary design teams of architects, landscape architects, engineers, horticulturists, lighting designers, and professionals from many other disciplines. The second competition resulted in four finalist teams, whose entries were displayed at the Center for Architecture in Greenwich Village.

TerraGRAM
From the proposal by TerraGRAM: Michael Van Valkenburgh Associates with D.I.R.T. Studio and Beyer Blinder Belle

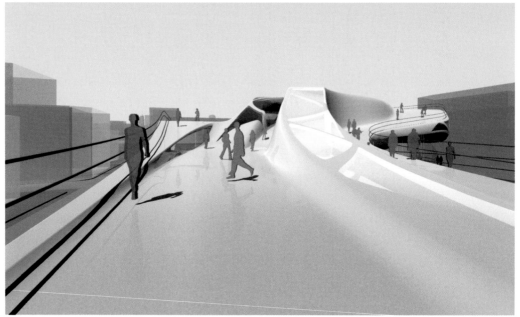

Zaha Hadid
From the proposal by
Zaha Hadid Architects
with Balmori Associ-
ates; Skidmore, Owings
and Merrill LLP; and
studioMDA

Steven Holl
From the proposal by
Steven Holl Architects
with Hargreaves
Associates and HNTB

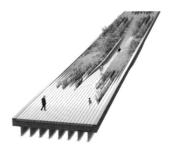

PIT
0% : 100%

PLAINS
40% : 60%

BRIDGE
50% : 50%

MOSSLAND

Dieranum
Leucobryum
Polytrichum
Thuidium

wet

TALL MEADOW

Avena
Festuca
Miscanthus
Pennisetum
Sorghastrum

dry

WETLAND

Aster
Carex
Epimedium
Luzula
Lythrum
Verbena

wet

MOUND
55% : 45%

RAMP
60% : 40%

FLYOVER
100% : 10%

WOODLAND THICKET

Adiantum spp.
Asarum
Betula nigra 'Heritage'
Clethra barbinervis
Sassafras albidum
Osmunda spp.
Viburnum dilitatum

wet/average

MIXED PERENNIAL MEADOW

Artemisia
Eryngium giganteum
Heuchera
Monarda
Persicaria
Sanguisorba officinalis
Salvia

dry/average

YOUNG WOODLAND

Agastache
Buxus sempervirens
Cercis canadensis
Lavatera
Rhus chinensis
Salix eleagnos

average

**James Corner Field
Operations and
Diller Scofidio + Renfro**
This winning proposal
grew into the High
Line's design as it exists
today.

what will grow here?

COMMUNITY

The High Line's design was created through a community-based process in which supporters, neighborhood residents, and other interested parties contributed input directly to the designers and Friends of the High Line.

opposite page
City Council Speaker
Christine C. Quinn
was one of the High
Line's first allies in City
government.

this page, top
City Planning Com-
mission Chair Amanda
Burden and Friends of
the High Line Board
Chair John Alschuler

this page, bottom
High Line capital
campaign leaders
Lisa Maria and Philip
Falcone

opposite page
Joshua David and
Robert Hammond with
Florent Morellet

this page, top
Joshua David, Diane
von Furstenberg, and
Robert Hammond at a
2003 fundraiser at the
DVF Studio.

The City had just
changed its policy to
one favoring the High
Line's reuse.

this page, bottom
Phil Aarons, Shelley
Fox Aarons, Robert
Hammond, and
Gifford Miller

opposite page
Members of the High
Line design team,
clockwise from upper
left: Matthew Johnson,
Charles Renfro, Lisa
Switkin, James Corner,

Nahyun Hwang,
Elizabeth Diller, and
Ricardo Scofidio

this page, top
Deputy Mayor for Eco-
nomic Development
and Rebuilding Daniel
Doctoroff speaks at
the High Line's ground-
breaking ceremony

this page, bottom
Edward Norton, Robert
Hammond, Joshua
David, and Kevin Bacon

GROUNDBREAKING
City Council Speaker Christine C. Quinn, Public Advocate
Betsy Gotbaum, Senators Hillary Rodham Clinton and Charles
E. Schumer, Mayor Michael R. Bloomberg, City Planning
Commission Chair Amanda M. Burden, and Congressman
Jerrold Nadler helped lift a railroad track at the High Line's
groundbreaking ceremony in April 2006.

CONSTRUCTION

The conversion of the High Line from a freight rail trestle into a park began in 2006 and required work in several stages. First grass, soil, rails and trestles, and other materials were removed. Next the site was repaired and waterproofed. Then the park environment, including pathways, access points, seating, lighting, planting-bed infrastructure, and plants, was put into place.

LANDSCAPE CONSTRUCTION

Many of the High Line's original railroad tracks were reinstalled into the new landscape. Tapered concrete planks were put in place, making up the High Line's pathway system.

opposite page
Landscape workers in
a planting bed above
West Thirteenth Street

this page
View, looking south, of
planting in the beds
below Fourteenth Street

HIGH LINE OPENS

On June 8, 2009, Section 1 of the High Line opened to the public following a ribbon-cutting ceremony.

GANSEVOORT PLAZA

The dramatic southern terminus of the High Line occupies the corner of Gansevoort and Washington Streets, complemented by a street-level public plaza and the High Line–level Gansevoort Overlook.

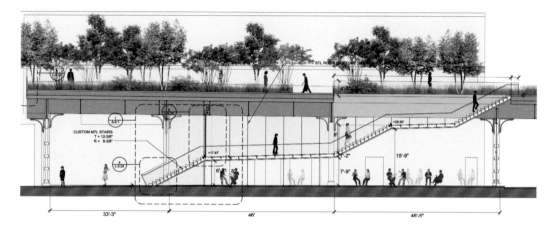

GANSEVOORT WOODLAND AND
WASHINGTON GRASSLANDS

The Gansevoort Woodland and Washington Grasslands
stretch for three blocks at the High Line's southern end,
terminating below the New York Standard Hotel.

above

An early architectural rendering of the Washington Grasslands shows the High Line's central design feature: a modular system of tapered concrete planks integrated into the planted areas.

LIGHTING

The High Line's lighting system was designed by L'Observatoire International. Rather than using traditional overhead lights, which can cause glare, the High Line's energy-efficient LED lights are incorporated into landscape elements such as benches and railings to gently illuminate pathways and planting beds.

WEST FOURTEENTH STREET

The High Line passes through the semi-enclosed former loading dock of what was once the Cudahy meatpacking plant before emerging over West Fourteenth Street.

DILLER–VON FURSTENBERG SUNDECK

With its spectacular river views, rolling lounge-chair seating, and water feature, the Sundeck is one of the most popular gathering places on the High Line. The water feature at this location, which creates a thin sheet of moving water on the walkway, is a popular spot for children.

CHELSEA MARKET PASSAGE

At West Fifteenth Street, the High Line passes through the former Nabisco bakery, now Chelsea Market. This passage is the site of much of Friends of the High Line's public programming, as well as *The River That Flows Both Ways*, an art installation by Spencer Finch in the windows of the passage.

NORTHERN SPUR PRESERVE

Crossing over Tenth Avenue to connect to a former refrigerated warehouse, the spur is home to naturalistic plantings
with great seasonal variation.

TENTH AVENUE SQUARE

At West Seventeenth Street, the High Line crosses Tenth Avenue and creates a dramatic square, the High Line's widest point. One of the park's most popular spots, the Tenth Avenue Square has amphitheater-like seating and cutout windows with a view up Tenth Avenue.

CHELSEA GRASSLANDS

Extending for three blocks as the High Line enters West Chelsea, the Chelsea Grasslands feature sun-loving grasses and perennial wildflowers, as well as spectacular views of the surrounding neighborhood's architecture.

CHELSEA THICKET

West Twentieth Street marks the beginning of the High Line's newest section, which opened in June 2011. Stretching two blocks north from this point, the Chelsea Thicket features a lush miniature forest of dogwoods, hollies, bottlebrush buckeye, roses, and other dense shrubs surrounding a meandering pathway.

SEATING STEPS AND WEST TWENTY-THIRD STREET LAWN

At West Twenty-second Street, stadium-style seating rises to meet the brick wall of a former warehouse west of the High Line. Slats of reclaimed teak fill in where a loading dock formerly stood, and create casual seating as the High Line widens to its broadest point in Chelsea. Here, the park's concrete pathway gives way to the lush grass of the Twenty-third Street Lawn. As it continues north, the lawn gently peels up from the surface of the High Line to create a subtly elevated vantage point with river-to-river views along Twenty-third Street.

opposite page
Warehouse buildings
block the High Line
from winds off the
river, and create a
sheltered area perfect
for lush planting.

LISA MARIA AND PHILIP A. FALCONE FLYOVER

As the High Line narrows to pass between two large
warehouse buildings, a grated metal walkway begins to lift
up from the surface of the High Line. The Falcone Flyover
reaches a height of eight feet, bringing visitors through a
canopy of bigleaf magnolia, sassafras, and serviceberry trees.
Shade-loving perennials and groundcovers fill in below the
walkway on the High Line's surface.

opposite page
Looking north at the
Falcone Flyover from
above Twenty-fourth
Street

259

WILDFLOWER FIELD

As the High Line approaches the northern edge of West Chelsea, the structure narrows. Here, the simplicity of a straight walkway with good sun exposure allows the High Line's horticulture to shine: perennial wildflowers bloom among green and golden grasses from early March to late October.

WEST THIRTIETH STREET CURVE
A long bank of radial benches follows the curve of the High
Line at West Thirtieth Street as it begins its gradual sweep
west toward the Hudson River. These benches provide a
social gathering spot near the High Line's current northern end,
and will soon serve as a transition to the rail yards section.

opposite page
View looking south;
the High Line is visible
from West Thirtieth
Street to West
Sixteenth Street.

WEST THIRTIETH STREET CUTOUT AND VIEWING PLATFORM

As the High Line passes above West Thirtieth Street, the structure's concrete decking has been removed, revealing a heavy latticework of structural steel and the pavement of the street below. A grated steel platform overlays the surface of the structure, providing views downward, as well as west toward the expanse of the Hudson River. A stair and elevator complete this feature, currently the northern terminus of the park.

DISTINCTIVE LANDSCAPE

The High Line's plantings, created by James Corner Field Operations with Piet Oudolf, is a constantly changing environment. More than 200 species of grasses, wildflowers, shrubs, and trees make up this one-of-a-kind landscape, which emphasizes seasonal variety, texture and color variation, and hardiness. A large percentage of the High Line's plants are native and drought-tolerant varieties.

this page, top
Planting designer
Piet Oudolf

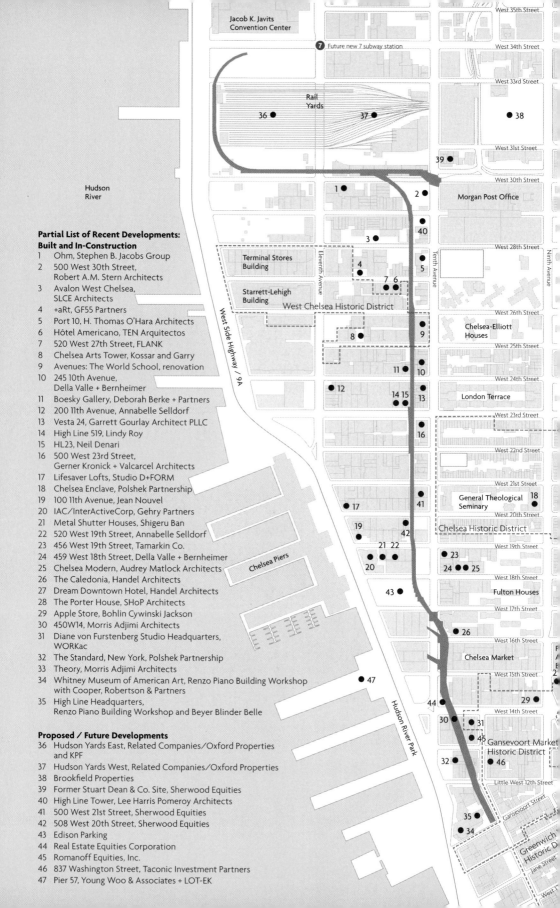

Partial List of Recent Developments:
Built and In-Construction

1 Ohm, Stephen B. Jacobs Group
2 500 West 30th Street,
  Robert A.M. Stern Architects
3 Avalon West Chelsea,
  SLCE Architects
4 +aRt, GF55 Partners
5 Port 10, H. Thomas O'Hara Architects
6 Hôtel Americano, TEN Arquitectos
7 520 West 27th Street, FLANK
8 Chelsea Arts Tower, Kossar and Garry
9 Avenues: The World School, renovation
10 245 10th Avenue,
  Della Valle + Bernheimer
11 Boesky Gallery, Deborah Berke + Partners
12 200 11th Avenue, Annabelle Selldorf
13 Vesta 24, Garrett Gourlay Architect PLLC
14 High Line 519, Lindy Roy
15 HL23, Neil Denari
16 500 West 23rd Street,
  Gerner Kronick + Valcarcel Architects
17 Lifesaver Lofts, Studio D+FORM
18 Chelsea Enclave, Polshek Partnership
19 100 11th Avenue, Jean Nouvel
20 IAC/InterActiveCorp, Gehry Partners
21 Metal Shutter Houses, Shigeru Ban
22 520 West 19th Street, Annabelle Selldorf
23 456 West 19th Street, Tamarkin Co.
24 459 West 18th Street, Della Valle + Bernheimer
25 Chelsea Modern, Audrey Matlock Architects
26 The Caledonia, Handel Architects
27 Dream Downtown Hotel, Handel Architects
28 The Porter House, SHoP Architects
29 Apple Store, Bohlin Cywinski Jackson
30 450W14, Morris Adjimi Architects
31 Diane von Furstenberg Studio Headquarters,
  WORKac
32 The Standard, New York, Polshek Partnership
33 Theory, Morris Adjimi Architects
34 Whitney Museum of American Art, Renzo Piano Building Workshop
  with Cooper, Robertson & Partners
35 High Line Headquarters,
  Renzo Piano Building Workshop and Beyer Blinder Belle

Proposed / Future Developments

36 Hudson Yards East, Related Companies/Oxford Properties
  and KPF
37 Hudson Yards West, Related Companies/Oxford Properties
38 Brookfield Properties
39 Former Stuart Dean & Co. Site, Sherwood Equities
40 High Line Tower, Lee Harris Pomeroy Architects
41 500 West 21st Street, Sherwood Equities
42 508 West 20th Street, Sherwood Equities
43 Edison Parking
44 Real Estate Equities Corporation
45 Romanoff Equities, Inc.
46 837 Washington Street, Taconic Investment Partners
47 Pier 57, Young Woo & Associates + LOT-EK

Jacob K. Javits Convention Center

Future new 7 subway station

Rail Yards

Hudson River

Morgan Post Office

Terminal Stores Building

Starrett-Lehigh Building

West Chelsea Historic District

Chelsea-Elliott Houses

London Terrace

General Theological Seminary

Chelsea Historic District

Chelsea Piers

Fulton Houses

Chelsea Market

West Side Highway / 9A

Hudson River Park

Gansevoort Market Historic District

Greenwich Historic D

West 35th Street
West 34th Street
West 33rd Street
West 31st Street
West 30th Street
West 28th Street
West 26th Street
West 25th Street
West 24th Street
West 23rd Street
West 22nd Street
West 21st Street
West 20th Street
West 19th Street
West 18th Street
West 17th Street
West 16th Street
West 15th Street
West 14th Street
Little West 12th Street
Gansevoort Street
Jane Street

Eleventh Avenue
Tenth Avenue
Ninth Avenue

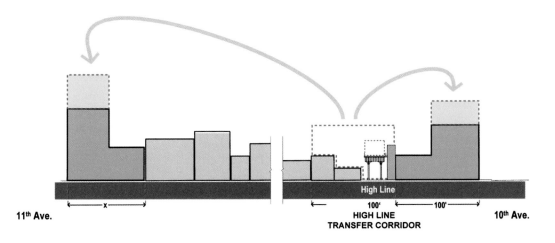

11ᵗʰ Ave.   HIGH LINE   10ᵗʰ Ave.
                          TRANSFER CORRIDOR

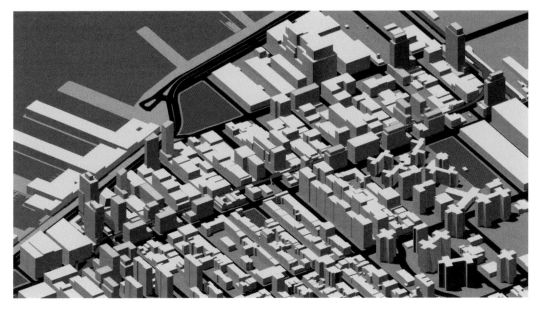

WEST CHELSEA REZONING

The Special West Chelsea district, which the city created in 2005, includes the blocks around the High Line. The rezoning allows for development rights hindered by the High Line's easement to be transferred from underlying properties to lots along Tenth and Eleventh Avenues.

opposite page
The Standard Hotel, at 848 Washington Street, by Polshek Partnership

this page, clockwise from top left
245 Tenth Avenue, by Della Valle Bernheimer

The Caledonia at 450 West Seventeenth Street, by Handel Architects

456 West Nineteenth Street, by Tamarkin Co.

450 West Fourteenth Street, known as the High Line Building. Addition by Morris Adjmi. The building sits on top of the historic former Cudahy packing plant.

NEW ARCHITECTURE

The commercial developments in the High Line neighborhood have given the area a reputation for innovative design.

this page, clockwise from top left
Metal Shutter Houses at 524 West Nineteenth Street, by Shigeru Ban Architects

100 Eleventh Avenue, by Jean Nouvel

Headquarters of IAC, by Gehry Partners

Diane von Furstenberg Studio Headquarters, by WORKac

opposite page
HL23 at 517 West Twenty-third Street, by Neil Denari

RAIL YARDS

One-third of the High Line runs around the perimeter of the West Side Rail Yards. This is one of the most spectacular sections of the High Line, offering sweeping views of the Midtown skyline and the Hudson River. The 26-acre Rail Yards themselves are slated for a large-scale residential and commercial development over the next ten years. There have been many development proposals for this site, some of which would have demolished part or all of the High Line. Friends of the High Line has continually advocated for the preservation of the entire historic High Line at the West Side Rail Yards.

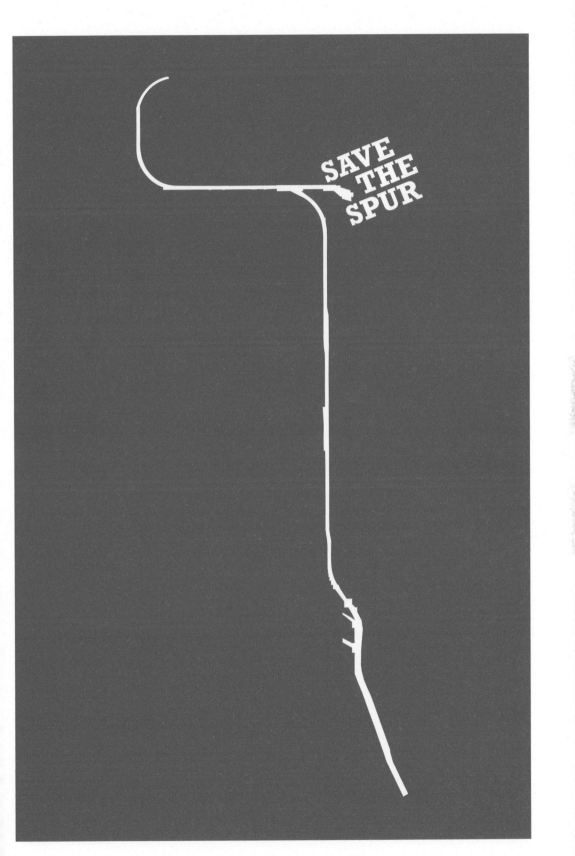

JETS STADIUM
An earlier plan for the rail yards included the building of a
new football stadium for the New York Jets. The stadium
was also intended to feature in New York's 2012 Olympic bid.
Plans for the stadium were called off in 2005.

RAIL YARDS DEVELOPMENT

In 2007, the Metropolitan Transportation Authority announced that it was soliciting bids for developers to lease the rights to build over the rail yards. The site was zoned to accommodate 12 million square feet of residential and commercial building, plus cultural facilities and public open space. The bidding process led to five developer proposals, some of which would have preserved the High Line while others would have demolished part or all of it.

this page
Extell Development Company. Architect: Steven Holl

opposite page
Brookfield Properties. Architects: Skidmore Owings & Merrill; Thomas Phifer & Partners; ShoP Architects; Diller Scofidio + Renfro; Kazuyo Sejima + Ryue Nishizawa; Handel Architects

HUDSON YARDS PLAN

The MTA selected the Related Companies to develop the West Side Rail Yards site. The planned development, called Hudson Yards, includes 12 million square feet of high-rise residential and commercial development, cultural facilities, and open space, and it incorporates the High Line.

both pages
2011 rendering and site plan for the Hudson Yards development proposal

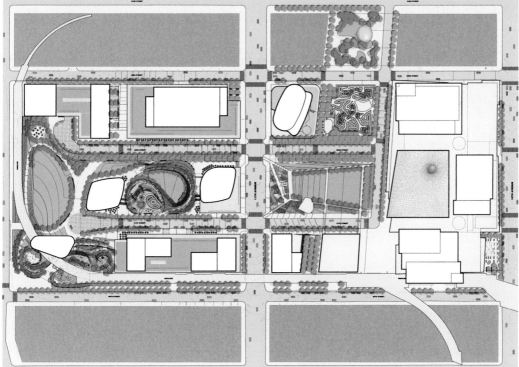

WHITNEY MUSEUM AND HIGH LINE HEADQUARTERS

The site adjacent to the High Line's southern terminus, at Gansevoort and Washington Streets in the Meatpacking District, is the future home of a branch of the Whitney Museum. The museum, designed by the Renzo Piano Building Workshop with Cooper, Robertson & Partners, is projected to open in 2015 (opposite page). The site will also house a maintenance and operations facility for the High Line (below).

PUBLIC PROGRAMMING

Friends of the High Line's free and low-cost public programs help to build a diverse, inclusive, and vibrant community around the High Line. Programs allow park visitors to learn more about the High Line's history and its recent transformation into a park. Programs also invite people to get inspired, to be active, and to enjoy the park together.

opposite page
Stargazing on the High
Line with the Amateur
Astronomers Associa-
tion of New York

this page
Students from the Har-
lem School of the Arts
learn about the history
of the High Line as
part of the High Line
field trip program.

this page
Students from PS 89 write down observations about the High Line as part of a field trip.

opposite page
Dancers of all ages perform in *Autumn Crossing*, Friends of the High Line's first commissioned dance piece, by Naomi Goldberg Haas Dances for a Variable Population, co-sponsored by the Hudson Guild.

A yoga class in the Chelsea Market Passage

HIGH LINE ART

High Line Art, Friends of the High Line's art program in partnership with the New York City Department of Parks & Recreation, places an emphasis on temporary site-specific pieces that respond to the uniqueness of the High Line.

this page
Kim Beck's *Space Available*, on rooftops adjacent to the High Line, 2011

opposite page
Richard Galpin's *Viewing Station*, on the High Line at Eighteenth Street, 2010

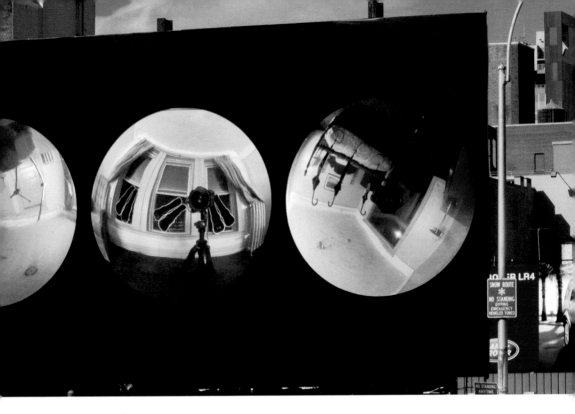

top
Billboard component
of Demetrius Oliver's
Jupiter, a multimedia
piece combining visual
art, performance, and
computer program-
ming, 2010

bottom
Spencer Finch's *The
River That Flows Both
Ways*, presented
in partnership with
Creative Time, in
the Chelsea Market
Passage, 2009

PARK OPERATIONS

Friends of the High Line's maintenance and operations staff includes gardeners, visitor services staff, technicians, custodians, and bathroom attendants, who keep the park running smoothly.

EPHEMERA

The High Line Renegade Cabaret performed frequently on an adjacent fire escape in the summer of 2009. Below, a portrait of Amanda Lepore, part of Michael Angelo's *Lipstick Portraits.*

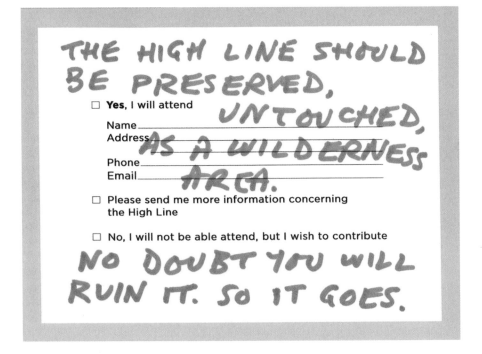

THE HIGH LINE SHOULD BE PRESERVED, UNTOUCHED, AS A WILDERNESS AREA.

□ **Yes**, I will attend

Name

Address

Phone

Email

□ Please send me more information concerning
the High Line

□ No, I will not be able attend, but I wish to contribute

NO DOUBT YOU WILL RUIN IT. SO IT GOES.

ACKNOWLEDGMENTS

As we set out to write this book, in late 2010, we were gearing up to open the second section of the High Line, from West Twentieth Street to West Thirtieth Street. The park would double in size, which meant we would have to hire new staff, get ready to maintain 50,000 new plants, expand our education and public programs, and grow our development and revenue departments to secure the funds we would need to take care of twice as much of the High Line. We had also just begun the first planning stages for the final section, at the West Side Rail Yards. It wasn't the ideal time to take on another project, but, for better or worse, we've established a pattern of often committing to more than sounds reasonable. Plus, we didn't think we'd be able to remember all the particulars of what happened ten years ago for much longer.

We set out to create a comprehensive visual overview of the High Line and to share some of the story of its transformation. At the same time, we hoped to dispel the idea that we began our ten-year journey to preserve, design, and build the High Line with some sort of overarching business plan or, really, any plan at all. As we've shown in these pages, we entered into this somewhat blindly. We relied heavily on the talents and good will of countless friends, government officials, creative professionals, board members, staffers, neighbors, donors, and volunteers, to whom we owe thanks.

All through December, we met each day with Katie Lorah, our former head of communications, whom we brought on to help us meet the book's tight deadlines. Katie interviewed us separately, mostly in our windowless, crowded back storage room—the only semi-soundproof space in our chaotic open office. The interviews were sometimes several hours long, and at times we strained to remember the order of legal developments, meetings, and turning points in our project. The interviews were then transcribed, resulting in reams of transcripts. We also dug up interviews from a 2005 oral history project that we'd never completed.

Josh was tasked with paring down these interviews into a single narrative, adding what we'd forgotten, and reframing what we'd remembered incorrectly. With the extraordinary guidance of Paul Elie at Farrar, Straus and Giroux, the story came together over months of early mornings and late nights, as Josh's writing and editing sandwiched his workday at the High Line office.

We're grateful to Paula Scher and Michael Schnepf at Pentagram, whose unfailing design elegance have turned our story into a literal thing of beauty. As the creators of our logo, our park signage, and many other materials throughout the years, Paula Scher and her colleagues at Pentagram have played a leading role in defining what the High Line is today.

We had been kicking around the idea of a book for a while, and it was Eliza Griswold, one of Robert's fellow Rome Prize recipients and a good friend, who introduced us to Jonathan Galassi, president and publisher of Farrar, Straus and Giroux.

We also acknowledge the leadership, personal commitment, and generosity of the many people—far too many to list here— who helped build the High Line itself. Without them, needless to say, there would be no book.

Standing at the forefront of this effort are the elected leaders who helped realize the High Line through their dedication of critical public funding. The High Line would not have been possible without the leadership of New York City Mayor Michael R. Bloomberg; City Council Speakers Christine C. Quinn and Gifford Miller; Manhattan Borough President Scott M. Stringer; U.S. Senators Charles E. Schumer, Hillary Rodham Clinton, and Kirsten Gillibrand; and U.S. Representative Jerrold L. Nadler.

We're grateful for the visionary leadership of our New York City partners: First Deputy Mayor Patricia E. Harris, Deputy Mayor for Economic Development Robert K. Steel and his predecessors Robert C. Lieber and Daniel L. Doctoroff, Economic Development Corporation President Seth W. Pinsky, Department of Parks & Recreation Commissioner Adrian Benepe, and City Planning Commission Chair Amanda M. Burden. We also gratefully acknowledge the guidance of the countless smart, dedicated people in New York City government as part of the Office of the First Deputy Mayor, Department of Parks & Recreation, Economic Development Corporation, Department of City Planning, Law Department, Mayor's Fund to Advance New York, Public Design Commission, Department of Buildings, Landmarks Preservation Commission, Mayor's Office for People with Disabilities, Mayor's Press Office, Department of Transportation, the New York City Council, the Office of the Manhattan Borough President, Manhattan Community Board No. 4, and Manhattan Community Board No. 2.

Crucial support at the New York State level came from Senator

Thomas K. Duane, as well as Assembly members Richard N. Gottfried and Deborah J. Glick.

It is with deep appreciation that we recognize our funding partners for their visionary support of the Campaign for the High Line, which supports construction of the new park and an endowment for its future maintenance and operations. The Diller–von Furstenberg Family Foundation and Philip A. Falcone and Lisa Maria Falcone have led this effort, and have lent their names to some of the High Line's most beloved features. Donald Pels and Wendy Keys, The Tiffany & Co. Foundation, The Pershing Square Foundation, Sherry and Douglas Oliver, the Hanson Family, Avenues: The World School, David Heller and Hermine Riegerl Heller, Michael and Sukey Novogratz, Elizabeth Belfer, Goldman Sachs, Google, The Philip and Janice Levin Foundation, Adam and Brittany Levinson, Christy and John Mack Foundation, and Catherine and Donald Marron—all have given New York a great gift with their support for key features on the High Line.

They are joined by John Blondel, The Bobolink Foundation and Wendy Paulson, Arland D. Williams, Jr., Philip E. Aarons and Shelley Fox Aarons, John Feinblatt and The Aber D. Unger Foundation, Lawrence B. Benenson, Nicholas Havard Bingham (1984–2004), James F. Capalino and Capalino+Company, Christopher and Sharon Davis, Barbaralee Diamonstein-Spielvogel, Kristen M. Dickey, Olivia Douglas and David DiDomenico, The Estée Lauder Companies, Inc. , Janet and Howard Kagan, Michael and Deborah McCarthy, Edward Norton, Elizabeth and Michael O'Brien, Mario J. Palumbo, Jr., Paul Pariser and Erin Leider-Pariser, Joelle and Jonathan Resnick, Steven Rubenstein, Joanne and Fred Wilson, Judith Zarin and Gerald Rosenfeld, and several supporters who wish to remain anonymous.

We are grateful for the donation of the High Line structure itself, which was generously given to the City of New York by CSX Transportation, Inc.

Our Board of Directors has been an essential force of guidance and support since the project's inception. There would be no High Line without founding Board Chair Philip Aarons, current Board Chair John Alschuler, and Board members Karen Ackman, Bruce Beal, John Blondel, James Capalino, Kristen Dickey, Bryan Eure, Lisa Maria Falcone, Philip Falcone, Janice Farber, Alexandre von Furstenberg, Gary Handel, Hermine Riegerl Heller, Eugene Keilin, Wendy Keys, Catherine Marron, Gifford Miller, Donald Mullen, Edward Norton, Mario Palumbo, Steven Rubenstein, Jason Stewart, Darren Walker, Joanne Wilson, Peter Wilson, and Bronson van Wyck. Emeritus Board members Vishaan Chakrabarti, Christopher Collins, Barbaralee Diamonstein-Spielvogel, Olivia Douglas, Elizabeth Gilmore, Robert Greenhood, Michael O'Brien, Esq., Richard Socarides, and Alan Stillman played key roles in the formation of the organization we have today. We gratefully acknowledge the crucial work of our Ex Officio Board members: Patricia E. Harris, Christine C. Quinn, Robert Steel, Adrian Benepe, and Amanda M. Burden.

We have the High Line's brilliant design team to thank for the beautiful park that visitors enjoy today. The team was led by James Corner, Lisa Switkin, and Nahyun Hwang of James Corner Field Operations; Liz Diller, Ric Scofidio, Charles Renfro, and Matthew Johnson of Diller Scofidio + Renfro; Piet Oudolf; Hervé Descottes of L'Observatoire International; Paula Scher of Pentagram Design, Inc.; Craig Schwitter of Buro Happold; and Joseph Tortorella of Robert Silman Associates.

The design team's ambitious visions were skillfully executed by a talented construction team led by LiRO/Daniel Frankfurt, SiteWorks, KiSKA Construction, and CAC Industries.

We're constantly amazed by our dedicated staff, who work day after day to operate the High Line and our organization to the highest standards. Many thanks to our current staff members: TJ Austin, Jeff Arnstein, Jordan Benke, Darryl Bowie, Dionne Broadus, Malik Brown, Roberto Castillo, Genevieve Chapin, Jennifer Chen, Gennaro Chierchio, Meriah Dainard, Kyla Dippong, Melissa Fisher, Logan Ford, Adam Ganser, AV Goodsell, Meg Graham, Jennifer Guilbert, John Gunderson, Patrick Hazari, Beth Heidere, Ben Holbrook, Joe Hsu, Stephen Jackson, Sanaya Kaufman, Alicia King, Enver Korenica, Mike Lampariello, Meagan Larkin, Sam Leonard, Louise Eddleston Lewis, Kate Lindquist, Johnny Linville, Rick Little, Nicole Melanson, DeLance Minefee, Kaaron Minefee, Daniel Mirisola, Michele Mirisola, Ambien Mitchell, Damien Moore, Tara Morris, Peter Mullan, Tone Murphy, Robert Newgarden, Patricia Ortiz, Karla Osorio-Pérez, Sean Patterson, Andi Pettis, Emily Pinkowitz, Anna Rahn, Tim Ries, Thomas Robertson, Brian Rodriguez, Peter Schmitz, Melina Shannon-DiPietro, Michelle Sharkey, Danya Sherman, Judith Simon, Kate Simpson, Ian Smith, John Speck, Jenny Staley, Maryanne Stubbs, Edward Styles, Hannah Toale, Maeve Turner, Michelle Udem, Miranda Varela, Neysha Vasquez, Max Waszak, Heather Wise, Kaspar Wittlinger, and Chris Wright.

And thanks to the former staff members who have contributed so much to help build our organization throughout the years: Julia Alschuler, Ben van Berkum, Harry Bissell, Julia Boyer, Suzy Brown, Alana Buckley, Jack Chan, Colleen Chisholm, Gardiner Comfort, Patrick Cullina, Kara Dove, Scott Dubois, Halima Duncan, Dahlia Elsayed, Auzelle Epeneter, Rachel Fields, Layna Fisher, Eliza Haburay-Herrling, Jeff Hafner, Deana Hare, J. C. Jogerst, Josh Karchem, Adam Kern, Salmaan Khan, Katie Lorah, Diane Nixa, Juliet Page, Pamela Reichen, Lynn Richardson, Justin Rood, Lauren Ross, James Russell, Edwin Sauls, Matthew Shakespeare, Andrew Shapiro, Dawson Smith, Olivia Stinson, Michael Swift, Chera Tappan, Meredith Taylor, and Howard Wai.

In addition, we gratefully remember the late Peter Obletz, railroad aficionado, community leader, Chelsea resident, and champion of the earliest movement to save the High Line.

Finally, we acknowledge the people who helped each of us personally as we worked on the High Line in the years since 1999.

JOSH

Thank you to my boyfriend of twenty-eight years, Stephen Hirsh. As I've worked on the High Line, Stephen has made all the tough parts easier and all the victories sweeter. I'm grateful for the support of my parents, John and Roberta David; my sister, Lisa David, my brother-in-law, Ernie Berger, my nieces, Nathalie and Claudia Berger; and Stephen's and my good friends Deborah Aschheim and Joyce Pierpoline. My grandparents, Charles David, Jeanne David, Terese David, and Josephine Delutis, all inspired me in different ways—there is a bit of each of them in the High Line. Special thanks go to the personal friends who became generous donors to the High Line, and to their counterparts, the generous donors to the High Line who became personal friends. I'm especially grateful to Robert—he could probably have made the High Line happen without me, but I could never have made the High Line happen without him.

ROBERT

I am grateful for the love and support of my entire family. My mother and dad always encouraged me to pursue my passions, no matter how offbeat. How many parents in Texas in the mid-eighties would help realize their teenager's dream to live in the USSR for a summer? My brother and sister still live in Texas, and though our lives are very different, I am thankful that they have included me in the wonderful families they've built.

As I mention in the text of the book, my longest-standing "partnership" has been with Josh, but I'm fortunate to have a string of ex-boyfriends who have become a de facto family for me. My first boyfriend, Scott Skey, with whom I first moved to the West Village in 1994, has remained a close friend and continues to help out with High Line events. And Nick Hosea, who I was with for much of the time period covered in this book, was and remains as passionate about the High Line as I have been.

Throughout the years I've spent on the High Line, I've been lucky to work alongside many close friends. In particular, I'd like to thank Gifford Miller, Phil Aarons, and Mario Palumbo, for their unfailing support of the High Line and, more important, for their friendship.

And lastly, thanks to Josh. Though this book is both our stories, it was Josh who was able to do what I could not and put it into words. Without his partnership, diligence, and great patience, there would be no High Line.

INDEX

Page numbers in *italics* refer to images.

Aarons, Phil: background, 9; as adviser to RH and JD, 9, 10, 11, 14, 17, 22, 23, 24, 41, 45, 75; on Friends of the High Line board, 14, 48; initial involvement with High Line project, 9, 10, 11, 14; photo, *185*; role in making High Line park a reality, 10, 13, 16, 25, 28, 34, 36, 44, 45, 71, 92, 115, 118; steps down as board chair, 116, 117; suggests Friends of the High Line name, 11; view on rail yards section of High Line, 102

Aarons, Shelley Fox, 9, 118, *185*

Ackman, Bill and Karen, 99, 104

Adjmi, Morris, 275

Alper, Andrew, 71

Alschuler, John: background, 45–46; photographed on High Line with Amanda M. Burden, *183*; presents study at community board hearing, 49; raises issues concerning operations side of High Line, 70, 110; role in design ideas competition, 53, 66; succeeds Phil Aarons as board chair of Friends of the High Line, 115, 116, 117; writes High Line's economic feasibility study, 46–47; writes High Line's rail yards studies, 102

Amateur Astronomers Association, 297

Amtrak, x

Andersen, Kurt, 76

Angelo, Michael, 313

AOL–Time Warner, 43

Architectural League, 16, 31

ARO architects, 74

Article 78 lawsuit, 36, 40, 42, 69

Automatic Slim's, 3

Bacon, Kevin, 27, 102, *187*

Balazs, André, 107

Balmori Associates, 74, 75, 173

Ban, Shigeru, 110, 276

Bargmann, Julie, 56, 67, 74

Bell Telephone Laboratories building, *140*

benches, park, 84

Benepe, Adrian, 71, 85, 117, 120

Bernhard, Sandra, 27

Berry, Halle, 113

Beyer Blinder Belle, 74, 170

Bingham, Edmund, 61

Blatchford, Laurel, 44, 54–55, 71, 82

Blondel, John, 98

Bloomberg, Michael R.: elected mayor, 40, 42, 44; at High Line groundbreaking, 97, *191*; at High Line ribbon cutting, 120, *200*; during mayoral campaign, 37–38, 40; support for High Line, 38, 40, 41, 42, 54, 69, 71, 78, 92, 98–99, 105

Board of Estimate, 36

Bohen Foundation, 59

Boone, Mary, 34, 35

Boss, Alan, 66

Botsford, Erik, 72

Bourscheidt, Randy, 61

Bridge of Houses proposal, x, 56, 74, 86, 151, *151*

Brookfield Properties, 108, 286

Brooklyn Bridge Park, 74

Brooklyn Bridge walkway, 85

Brooklyn Heights, 85

Bryant Park, 71

Burden, Amanda M.: background, 29; becomes chair of City Planning Commission, 42, 43; connection to Mark Green, 29, 38, 40, 42; at High Line groundbreaking, 97, *191*; at High Line ribbon cutting, 120; as member of City Planning Commission, 29, 40, 42, 43, *183*; RH's introduction to, 29; support for High Line, 29, 32, 35, 41, 43, 44, 64, 72, 74, 84, 89, 90, 97, 99, 106, 117; and Vishaan Chakrabarti, 57, 64, 112

Bush, George W., 56, 111

Cablevision, 86, 88

Caledonia, The, 97–98, 275

Calvin Klein Collection anniversary, 113

Capalino, Jim, 30, 37, 42, 44, 45, 66, 87

Capehart, Jonathan, 38, 40, 42

capital campaign, 51, 81–82, 98, 103–104, 113, 114–15, 117

Carfrae, Malcolm, 113

Caro, Robert, 61

Caviar Russe, 26, 81

Center for Architecture, 76, 170

Central Park Conservancy, 42, 70–71, 110

Certificate of Interim Trail Use (CITU), 16–17, 54, 70, 82, 89–90

Chakrabarti, Vishaan, 57, 64, 65, 78, 112

Chelsea-Elliott Houses, 51, 103, 107

Chelsea Grasslands, *242*, 243, *243*, *244–45*, 246, *247*

Chelsea Market, 11–12, 44, 118–19, 230, *230*, *231*, *232–33*, *299*, *302–303*

Chelsea neighborhood, 3–4, 5, 6, 15, 19–21, 64–66; *see also* West Chelsea

Chelsea Plan, 21

Chelsea Property Owners, x, xi, 19, 43, 49, 53, 54, 64, *158–59; see also* Sarini, Doug

Chelsea Thicket, *248,* 249, *249*

Cheney, Dick, 111

Christo and Jean-Claude, 34

Church of the Guardian Angel, 4, 20

Ciabotti, Jeff, 16, 31

Cipriani Wall Street, 90

CITU, *see* Certificate of Interim Trail Use (CITU)

City Planning Commission, *see* New York City, Planning Commission

Cleater, John, 163

Clemente, Francesco, 55

Clinton, Hillary, 62, 81, 90, 91; at High Line groundbreaking, 97, *190*

Cohen, Irwin, 12

Colicchio, Tom, 114

Collins, Chris, 28, 36, 37, 42, 48

Committee of the Whole (COW), City Hall, 45

community board: CSX presentation at Penn South meeting, 7; introducing Friends of the High Line to local boards, 14–15; JD joins local board, 34, 52–53, 57; neighborhood hearing about Friends of the High Line, 19–21; Preservation and Planning Committee, 5; RH and JD first meet at Penn South meeting, 7, 153; seeking Board 4's support, 49, 57

Compton, Lee, 57

conditional abandonment order, 10, 17

Coney Island, 41

Congestion Mitigation and Air Quality (CMAQ), 81

Conrail (Consolidated Rail), x, xi

conservancies, 108, 110–11, 117; *see also* Central Park Conservancy; Rails-to-Trails Conservancy

Cooke, Lynnets, 57

Cooper, Anderson, 90

Cooper, Paula, 4, 15, 22, 36

Corner, James, 74, 75, 84, 91, *186; see also* Field Ops/DS+R

Corwin, Carolyn, 82

Costa, Anisa Kamadoli, 106

Covington and Burling, 25, 66, 82

Creative Time, 29, 92–93

Cross, Jay, 67

CSX Transportation, Inc., xi, 6, 7, 10–11, 18, 23, 38, 50, 70, 79, 93, 108, 127, 154; *see also* Frank, Debra

Cudahy meatpacking plant, *220,* 221, 275

Cullina, Patrick, 111, 120

Cunningham, Bill, 35

Cuti, John, 36, 48, 50

David, Joshua (JD): background, 3–4, 5, 6; comparison with RH, 10, 21; first meets RH, xi, 7, 8, 153; first taken up to see High Line, 11–12; at High Line ribbon cutting, 120–21, *200;* initial interest in

saving High Line, 6; joins local community board, 34, 52–53, 57; as New Year's 2000, 18; as officer in Friends of the High Line, 14; photos, *153,* *184,* *185,* *187;* presentation of economic feasibility study to City, 52–53; relationship with RH, 23–24, 59, 60, 62–63; testifies about High Line at community board hearing, 19–21; testifies at City Council hearing, 32

Davis, Rich, 110

De Feo, Michael, 96

Delanoë, Bertrand, 44

Della Valle Bernheimer, 275

demolition: arguments in favor, 7, 19–21; and Bloomberg's mayoral campaign, 37–38, 40; holding off, 28–29, 31–32, 39–40; lawsuit opposing, 25, 27, 34, 36–38, 40, 42, 48–49, 69; partial, south of Gansevoort Street, ix, xi, 6; proponents, 10–11, 13, 19–21, 25, 40, 41, 42, 83

Denari, Neil, 107, 276

Descottes, Hervé, 125; *see also* lighting

design competition, 73–80, 170, *170–77; see also* Field Ops/DS+R; ideas competition

Design Trust for Public Space, 24, 29–30, 34, 38–39, 42–43, 66

development, 23–24, 30, 272; *see also* Economic Development Corporation (EDC); fund-raising, Friends of the High Line; Hudson Yards Development Commission (HYDC); West Side Rail Yards, proposed development plans

development rights, 23, 52, 64, 65, 70, 89, 273, *273*

Dia Center for the Arts, 4, 37, 87, 88, 100

Diamonstein-Spielvogel, Barbaralee, 72, 76, 90, 91, 102

Diller, Barry: attends MoMA design team exhibition, 91; cohosts High Line preview dinner, 118, 119; commissions Frank Gehry to design IAC headquarters building, 103, 106; family decisions about donations, 93, 94; at High Line groundbreaking, 96; at High Line ribbon cutting, 120; meets with JD and RH about economic downturn, 114–15; notifies JD and RH of family's $10 million challenge gift, 115

Diller, Elizabeth, 75, 91, 104, *186*

Diller Scofidio + Renfro: as design team finalist, 74, 75, 76, 77–78, 176, *176,* *177;* in Miss Meat Market Gown competition, 92; offices, 83, 104; selected as part of Field Ops/DS+R team, 78, 83; staff member in charge, 83

Diller–von Furstenberg Sundeck, 118, 119, 125, 224, 225–29; *see also* Diller, Barry; von Furstenberg, Diane

Dinkins, David, 40–41

direct mail, 109

D.I.R.T. Studio, 74, 170

Dirty Martini, 92

Doctoroff, Dan: background, 44, 45; first meets with Friends of the High Line, 44–45; at High Line groundbreaking, *187;* at MoMA High Line exhibition opening party, 86; and New York bid for 2012 Olympics, 44, 45, 46, 52, 65, 67, 68; office cooperates with High Line project, 54–55, 62, 64, 69–70, 79, 82–83, 86; and rail yards planning process, 46–47, 52, 53, 67, 68, 69–70, 86, 105, 106; receives High Line economic feasibility study, 49, 52–53; and stadium issue, 46–47, 52, 53, 65, 67–68, 69–70, 86; on steering committee to select design team, 71

dot-com boom, 13

Douglas, Olivia, 14, 26, 32, 72

Duane, Tom, 15

Duane Park, 46

Dunlap, David, 54

Durso, Robert, 36

Durst, Douglas, 105, 108, 109

Durst, Helena, 109

Dutch Bulb Association, 120

easements, rail, ix, x, 6, 16, 37, 68, 70, 273

Easterling, Keller, 29

Economic Development Corporation (EDC), 9, 71, 72, 80, 92

economic feasibility study, 45, 49, 52–53, 98, 102, 115

Edison Properties, 43, 64, 65

eGroups, 19

Eleey, Peter, 92, 93

elevated walkways, DOT requirement, 85

Elsayed, Dahlia, 33, 43

Emery, Richard, 28, 36, 48

Empire State Building, relationship to High Line, 32, 33

Extell Development, 108–109, 286

Falco, Edie, 61

Falcone, Philip and Lisa, 99, 104, 112, 119, 120, *183*, 255; *see also* Flyover feature

Falk, Jennifer, 96

Fashion Week, 113

fences, 85

Ferrer, Fernando "Freddie," 28, 37

Field Ops/DS+R, *186*; chosen to create High Line landscape, 78, 83; as design team finalist, 74, 75, 76, 77–78, *176*, *176*, *177*; overview of High Line landscape, 266, *266–71*; and Piet Oudolf, 74, 77, 111, 120, 269; *see also* Corner, James

Fields, C. Virginia, 28, 37

Fisher, Melissa, 111, 120

Fitzmaurice, Sara, 37

Florent (restaurant), *see* Morellet, Florent

Flotilla DeBarge, 91

Flower District, 21

Flyover feature, 77, 114, *254*, 255, *255–59*

Forsythe, William, 92

foundation grants, 47, 51, 106

Fourteenth Street, *222–23*

Frank, Debra, 6, 10, 11–12, 13, 23, 50

Frederick, Pam, 19

Friedman, Howard, 83

Friends of the High Line: board members, 14, 48–49, 115–17; as bottom-up project, 127; choosing name, 11; as conservancy, 117; economic feasibility study, 45, 49, 52–53, 98, 102, 115; first brochure, 22; founding, 3–16, 153, *153*; future goals, 129; impact of 9/11 attacks on High Line project, 39–40; initial planning study, 24–25, 29–30, 38–39, 42–43; logo, 17, *152*, *178*, *314*, *315*; office space for project, 33–34, 51; public programming, 126, 294, *294–99*; RFQ for design team, 73–74; *see also* David, Joshua; design competition; fund-raising, Friends of the High Line; Hammond, Robert

Front Studio, 58, 169

Fulton Houses, 19, 51, 64, 103, 107

fund-raising, Friends of the High Line: advice from Phil Aarons, 22, 45; capital campaign, 51, 81–82, 98, 103–104, 113, 114–15, 117; events, 26–27, 34–35, 55, 108, 113; hiring of Juliet Page, 51–52

furniture, park, 84

Gansevoort Plaza, *204*, 205, *205*, *206*, *207*, *290*, 291, *291*; *see also* Whitney Museum

Gansevoort Street, xi, 6

Gansevoort Woodland, 208, *208–209*, *210*, *211*, *214–15*

Garvin, Alex, 67

Gastil, Ray, 18

gayness, 35–36

Gehry, Frank, 103, 106, 110, 276

Gilman, Rowann, 37

Gilmore, Elizabeth, 22

Giuliani, Rudy, 5, 13, 25, 28, 29, 40

Gladstone, Barbara, 4

Gladwell, Malcolm, 127

Goldman Sachs, 98

Google, 19, 128

Gopnik, Adam, 32, 38

Gottesman, Jerry, 65, 90

Govan, Michael, 87–88, 100

Gramercy Park, 46

Grand Central Terminal, 23, 58, 59, 60, 64, *169*

Grand Chelsea, 21

grasses, *see* Chelsea Grasslands; Washington Grasslands

Graves, Michael, 100

Greco, Len, 72

Green, Mark, 28, 29, 38, 40, 42

Greenacre Foundation, 47

Greenbelt Native Plant Center, 100

Greenblack paint, 99

Gulotta, Tony, 37

Gunn, Joe, 83

Ha, Yen, 51, 58

Haas, Naomi Goldberg, 298

Hadid, Zaha, 74, 75, 173

Hamilton, Jo, 47, 48, 63, 87

Hammond, Robert (RH): background, 3, 4, 5; comparison with JD, 10, 21; decision to take salary for Friends of the High Line work, 49–50; first meets JD, xi, 7, 8, 153; first taken up to see High Line, 11–12; at High Line ribbon cutting, 121, *200*; initial interest in saving High Line, 5; as officer in Friends of the High Line, 14; photos, *153, 184, 185, 187*; presentation of economic feasibility study to City, 52–53; relationship with JD, 23–24, 59, 60, 62–63; testifies about High Line at community board hearing, 19–21; testifies at City Council hearing, 32

Handel, Gary, 14, 16, 26, 43, 71, 72, 110, 275

Hansen, Laura, 19

Hargreaves Associates, 74, 175

Hariri sisters, 57

Harris, Patricia E., 71, 78, 121

Hart, Kitty Carlisle, 61

Hearst, Patty, 61

Hector's, 87, *292*

Heffley, Patty, 126

Heller, David and Hermine, 99, 104

Hemmer, Mike, 25, 27, 82

High Line, as railroad structure: arguments for tearing down, 7, 19–21, 43, *158, 159*; end of train traffic, x, *146, 147, 147, 148, 149*; history, viii–xi, *134–47*, 135, 136, 138, 141, 145, 147; as Lifeline of New York, 145; proposals for reuse, xi, 7, 8, 29, 31, 42, 70, 89; as relic of another time, 6; structural integrity assessment, 49; train tracks through buildings, *140, 141, 141*

High Line, reuse as park: aerial view from Thirtieth Street to Sixteenth Street, *264*; art program, 300, *300, 301, 302–303*; Chelsea Grasslands, *242, 243, 243, 244–45, 246, 247*; design as community-based process, 95–96, 178; design competition, 73–80, 170, *170–77*; Flyover feature, 77, 114, *254, 255, 255–59*; Gansevoort Woodland, 208, *208–209, 210, 211, 214–15*; groundbreaking ceremony, 96–97, *187, 190–91*; ideas competition, 53–61, *162–69*, 163; landscape, 196, *196–99*, 266, *266–71*; lighting, 125, *216, 217, 218, 219, 219*; map of recent developments, *272*; neighborhood map painting, *188–89*; new neighborhood architecture, *272, 274, 275, 275, 276, 277*; Northern Spur Viewing Preserve, 85, *234, 235, 235, 318–19*; operations and maintenance, 109–11, *304, 305, 305, 306–307, 308, 309*; popularity of park, 125; as relic of another time, 6; section 1 ribbon-cutting ceremony, 120–21, *200–201*; site preparation work, 94–101; southern terminus, *204, 205, 205, 206, 207, 290, 291, 291, 292–93*; Sundeck feature, 118, 119, 125, 224, *225–29*; Tenth Avenue Square, 31, 85, 104, *132–33, 236–39, 237*; Thirtieth Street curve, *262, 262, 263*; time line, viii–xi; transformation from freight rail trestle into park, *192, 192–99*; walking tour, *202–15*; Washington Grasslands, 208, *208–209, 210, 211, 212–13*; Wildflower Field, 260, *260–61*; *see also* Friends of the High Line

High Line Building, *275*

High Line Park Association, 8, 11

High Line Portrait Project, 107–108, *179–81*

High Line Reality flyers, 43, *158, 159*

High Line Renegade Cabaret, 126, *312*

Hill, Murray, 91

Hitchcock, Jim, 59

HL23 (condominium tower), *277*

Hock, Karen, 39

Holl, Stephen: Bridge of Houses design, x, 56, 74, 86, 151, *151*; designs Extell's rail yards proposal, 108–109; as finalist in design competition, 74–75, *76–77*, 175; on jury for ideas competition, 56

Holland, Sarah, 110

Hoppa, Jennifer, 72

Hudson Guild, 51, 57, 62, 68, 298

Hudson River Park, 57, 74

Hudson Yards, 288; rendering and site plan, *288–89*; *see also* West Side Rail Yards

Hudson Yards Community Advisory Committee, 106

Hudson Yards Development Commission (HYDC), 101–102, 104–105

Hwang, Nahyun, *186*

IAC (InterActiveCorp) building, 103, 106, *276*

ICC, *see* Interstate Commerce Commission (ICC)

ideas competition, 53–61, *162–69*, 163; *see also* design competition

InterActiveCorp (IAC) building, 103, 106, *276*

Interstate Commerce Commission (ICC), x, xi, 10

Iovine, Julie, 76

iterative processes, 24

Izes, Laurie, 50, 75, 127

Jacobs, Jane, 73, 97

Jean-Claude, *see* Christo and Jean-Claude

JM Kaplan Fund, 47

Johnson, Matthew, 83, *186*

Jones, Casey, 29–30, 34, 38, 39, 56

Jones, Richard, 169

Kaminer, Ariel, 76

Kaufman, Sanaya, 109

Kellogg, Fernanda, 106

Keys, Wendy, 26, 47, 81, 82, 110–11, 117

"King's Dream of New York" illustration, *137*

Kingsley, Mark, 37

Kirkland, Ed, 5, 6, 11, 21, 23

Kitchen, The, 4, 31, 104

Kletecka, Tom, 107–108

Koch, Ed, 9, 30

Kohn Pedersen Fox, 67

Koolhaas, Rem, 74, 100

Kroloff, Reed, 56

Kuhlmann, Ruth, 47
Kulikowski, Bob, 28, 37
Kustow, Lionel, 23

LaForce, James, 26, 120
Laird, Joshua, 72
Landmark West, 37
Landmarks Preservation Commission, 63
Latz, Peter, 73–74
Lauer, Scott, 67
lawn, *see* Twenty-third Street Lawn
Lehman Brothers, 113
Leibovitz, Annie, 93
Leport, Amanda, *313*
Levin, Anna, 106
Levin, Brenda, 28
Levinson, Brittany and Adam, 104
"Lifeline of New York," 145
lighting, 125, *216, 217, 218,* 219, *219*
Lignano, Giuseppe, 59
Lincoln Highway, 9
Lipstick Portraits, 313
Little, Rick, 55, 56
L'Observatoire International, 125, 219
logo, Friends of the High Line, 17, *152, 178, 314, 315*
London Terrace, 28
Lorah, Katie, 95
LOT-EK architects, 58–59
Loven, Zazel, 37

Maazel, Ilann, 36
Madonna, 91
Manzer, Jeff, 79, 92
maps, High Line: Paula Scher painting, *188–89*; recent developments, *272*
Marks, Matthew, 4, 15
Mastro, Randy, 25
Matta-Clark, Gordon, 93
McCall, Dirk, 30
McGuire, Janice, 51
Meatpacking District, 4, 47, 48, 63, 64, 69, 87, 91, 110, 291, *291*
Meier, Richard, 15, 22
Meloni, Luisella, 55
Merchant's Refrigerated Warehouse, *141*
Merck Family Fund, 47
Metal Shutter Houses, *276*
Metropolitan Pavilion, 66
Meyers, Jon, 46
Miller, Gifford: background, 5; as City Council speaker, 41, 44, 53–54, 60, 71–72, 89, 94, 99–100; help acknowledged, 14, 117, 118; at High Line groundbreaking, 97; as member of City Council, 5, 28, 37; photo, *185*
Miller, Lynden, 16, 22, 32, 41
Miller Elevated Highway, 138
MoMA (Museum of Modern Art), 85–86, 91
money shot, 18
Morellet, Florent, 35, 47–48, 55, 63, 76, 91, *184*
Morris, Tara, 109
Moss, Murray, 57
Mullan, Peter, 72, 106
Municipal Art Society, 15, 16, 19, 23, 27, 43
Muschamp, Herbert, 75, 78
Museum of Modern Art, 85–86, 91
Muz, Julie Atlas, 92

Nabisco bakery, 12, 230
Nadler, Jerry, 22, 62, 70, 81, 90–91, 105; at High Line groundbreaking, 97, *191*; at High Line ribbon cutting, 120, *200*
Naman, Alf, 107
National Trails System Act, x, 16
Neighborhood Preservation Center, 33
New York, New York: bid for 2012 Olympics, 30, 44, 45, 46, 52, 65, 67, 68, 88; past futuristic views, 136, *136, 137*; street-level railroad tracks, viii–ix, *134*, 135, *135*; West Side history, viii–xi, *134*, 135, *135*; *see also* New York City government
New York Central Elevated Spur, 138, *138, 139*
New York Central Railroad, viii–x, *135*, 142, *143*, 145
New York City Council: allocates funds to High Line, 60; High Line hearing, 31–32; Members' Lounge, 45; Miller elected speaker, 41; Quinn elected speaker, 94; winning over, 28–29, 37; *see also* Miller, Gifford; Quinn, Christine
New York City Economic Development Corporation (EDC), 9, 71, 72, 80
New York City government: 2001 mayoral race, 37–38, 40, 42, 44; Department of City Planning, 36, 57, 64, 84, 89, 97, 112; files for Certificate of Interim Trail Use for High Line, 54; Friends of the Highline lawsuit against, 25, 27, 34, 36–38, 40, 42, 48–49, 69; High Line on official City Map, 37; Parks Department, 85, 100, 110, 117; Planning Commission, 13, 28, 29, 30, 38, 42, 43; receives Certificate of Interim Trail Use for High Line, 89–90; supporters of High Line with influence in Bloomberg administration, 42; *see also* New York City Council
New York Jets stadium, 67–68, 73, 80, 87, 88, *285*
New York magazine, 106–107
New York State, 79, 102
New York Times, The, 5, 6, 13, 35, 42, 54, 76, 78–79, 89, 118, 126
New Yorker, The, 32, 38
New Yorkers for Parks, 47, 51
Nielsen, Signe, 56–57

9/11 attacks, 39–40

Nixa, Diane, 48, 103, 106, 109, 110

Nober, Roger, 62

Northern Spur Preserve, 85, *234*, 235, *235*, *318–19*

Norton, Edward, Jr., 33, 50–51, 61, 104, 105, *187*

Norton, Edward, Sr., 33, 90

Nouvel, Jean, 107, 110, 276

Novogratz, Mike and Sukey, 31, 99, 104

Obletz, Peter, x, 20, 22, *150*, 151

Oliver, Doug, 31

Olympics, New York's 2012 bid, 30, 44, 45, 46, 52, 65, 67, 68, 88

Onassis, Jackie, 23

Open House New York, 67, 80, 86, 108

OpenMeshWork, 73

Ortenzio, James, 87, 88

Oudolf, Piet, 74, 77, 111, 120, *269*

Ouroussoff, Nicolai, 78–79

Pace/McGill gallery, 38

Padovani, Jen, 98

Page, Juliet, 47, 51–52, 56, 81, 82, 85–86, 90, 103, 109

paint, Greenblack, 99

Paley, Babe, 29

Palumbo, Mario, 9, 10, 14, 19, 28, 36

Paris, France: mayor views High Line at rail yards, 44; Promenade Plantée, 14, 56, 84

Park restaurant, The, 35

Parks Department, *see* New York City government, Parks Department

Parsons, Brinckerhoff engineering firm, 47

passeggiata, 126

Pasternak, Anne, 92

Pawson, John, 113

Pels, Donald, 26, 47, 71, 81, 82, 110–11

Penn Central, x

Penn South complex, 7

Penn Station, x, 105

Pentagram, 17, 42, 59

Phillips de Pury auction house, 76, 98

Piano, Renzo, 100

Pierpoline, Joyce, 14

Pitt, Brad, 51

Planning Commission, *see* New York City government, Planning Commission

Pogrebin, Robin, 118

Polshek Partnership, 57, 72, 107, 275

Port Authority, 34

Portrait Project, 107–108, *179–81*

Preli, Richard, 169

Preservation League of New York State, The, 43

Princeton Architectural Press, 22

Promenade Plantée, Paris, 14, 56, 84

Public Authorities Control Board, 88

public-private partnership, 71

Quinn, Christine: background, 15, 94; becomes City Council speaker, 94; at High Line groundbreaking, 97, *190*; at High Line ribbon cutting, 120, *200*; as local City Council member, 15, 28, 31, 34, 89, 94; support for High Line, 22, 102, 106, *182*

Radical Faeries, 43, 79

railbanking, x, 16–17, 33, 47, 54, 68, 70, 79

railroads, *see* CSX Transportation, Inc.; High Line, as railroad structure; New York Central Railroad

Rails-to-Trails Conservancy, 6, 7, 16, 31, 33, 90

rail yards, *see* West Side Rail Yards

Randall's Island Sports Foundation, 110

Rawhide, 62

real estate, *see* Chelsea Property Owners; development rights

Regional Plan Association, xi, 7

Related Companies, The, 97, 108, 112–13, 288

Renfro, Charles, 104, *186*; *see also* Diller Scofidio + Renfro

Request For Qualifications (RFQ), 73–74, 170

Restuccia, Joe, 57

rezoning, 52–53, 64–66, 82–83, 89, 90, 98, 273, *273*

ribbon cutting, 120–21, *200–201*

Richards, Dave, 10

Ricks, Marc, 71, 79, 82–83

Rider, Peter, 28, 34

Riggio, Len, 100

rights transfer system, *see* development rights

Riley, Terry, 86

Rinne, Nathalie, 58, 163

Rock, Michael, 57, 74

Rockrose Development Corporation, xi

Rogers, Betsy Barlow, 42, 70

Rood, Justin, 55, 56

Rose, Joe, 13, 30, 65, 90, 106

Roskoff, Allen, 38

Rouse, James, 33

Roxy Nightclub, 35, 91–92

Rudakevych, Ostap, 51, 58

Saarinen, Eero, 43

Sachs, 34

Sahlman, Will, 26

Sanchis, Frank, 16

Sarini, Doug, 7, 19

Save Gansevoort Market project, 47, 48, 55, 63

Schenendorf, Jack, 66

Scher, Paula, 17, 42, 59; neighborhood map painting, *188–89*

Schliemann, Todd, 107

Schoormans, Lucas, 26

Schumer, Chuck, 62, 81, 91; at High Line ground breaking, 97, *190*

Scofidio, Ric, 77, 91, 104, *186*

Sedgwick, Kyra, 27

Selldorf, Annabelle, 110

September 11 attacks, 39–40

"Seven to Save" preservation campaign, 43

Sherman, Danya, 126

Sherwin-Williams, 99

Shields, Brooke, 113

Shorter, Charles, 34

Skey, Scott, 26, 81

Skidmore, Owings and Merrill, 34, 56, 75, 173

Smith, Nanette, 78

Socarides, Richard, 25, 28, 42–43

Speyer, Rob, 112

Spitzer, Eliot, 102

St. John's Park Terminal, ix

Standard Hotel, 64, 107, 117, 120, 126–27, 208, *209, 274*

Starrett-Lehigh Building, 50, 57, 59, 60, 83

STB, *see* Surface Transportation Board (STB)

Steidl, Gerhard, 38

Sternbergh, Adam, 106

Sternfeld, Joel: asked to photograph High Line wildscape, 18, 22; donates photos for fund-raising events, 26, 34; featured in *New Yorker* article, 32; Friends of the High Line features his photos, 26, 32, 42, 45, 59, 86, 93, *154, 155, 156–57*; honored at High line summer benefit, 90; at mayor's cultivation dinner, 99; photo as backdrop for High Line Portrait Project, 107, *179–81*; shows photos at Pace/McGill gallery, 38; significance of his High Line photos, 32; *Walking the High Line* series of photographs, 38, 108, *154, 155, 156–57*

Stewart, Martha, 50, 51

Stinson, Olivia, 55

Stringer, Scott, 99–100, 120

studioMDA, 173

Sundeck, 118, 119, 125, 224, *225–29*

Surface Transportation Board (STB), 10, 17, 27, 54, 62, 66, 89

Switkin, Lisa, 83, *186*

Tachibana, Ed, 26, 43

Tamarkin Co., 275

Taylor, Marilyn Jordan, 34, 56, 75

Taylor, Meredith, 108

Teardrop Park, 74

Tenth Avenue Square, 31, 85, 104, *132–33, 236–39, 237*

TerraGRAM, 170

Theater District, 23, 64

Theroux, Justin, 61

Thirtieth Street: aerial view of High Line south to Sixteenth Street, *264*; curve, *262, 262, 263*; cut-out and viewing platform, 114, *265, 265*

Tiffany & Co. Foundation, 106

Tishman Speyer, 108, 112

Tolla, Ada, 59

Trail Use Agreement, 93

Tschumi, Bernard, 56

Turner Construction, 49

Turrell, James, 113

TWA terminal at Kennedy Airport, 43

Twenty-third Street Lawn, 250, *250, 251, 252–53*

ULURP (Uniform Land Use Review Procedure), 36, 37, 42, 117

under-the-fence tours, 50–51

Vallone, Peter, 28, 37

Van Alen Institute, 16, 18

Van Valkenburgh, Michael, 74, 170

Van Wyck, Bronson, 26, 27, 35, 55

Vanderbilt, Cornelius, viii

Vanderbilt Hall, Grand Central Terminal, 58, 59, 60, *169*

von Furstenberg, Alex: background, 35, 93; as Friends of the High Line board member, 91, 115, 117; RH describes meeting for the first time, 35

von Furstenberg, Diane: attends MoMA design team exhibition, 91; cohosts High Line preview dinner, 118, 119; description of West 12th Street office, 93; family offers $5 million dollar High Line donation, 93–94, 96; family offers $10 million High Line challenge gift, 115; at High Line groundbreaking, 96; at High Line ribbon cutting, 120, *201*; as High Line summer benefit honoree, 102; hosts fund-raising dinner at IAC building, 103; hosts preview of High Line design team finalist exhibition, 76; hosts studio fund-raiser for Friends of the High Line, 55, *185*; JD describes meeting for the first time, 35; as mother of Alex von Furstenberg, 35; studio headquarters building, *276*; as supporter of Save Gansevoort Market project, 47, 55

von Furstenberg, Tatiana, 93, 115

Vornado Realty Trust, 105, 108, 109

***Walking the High Line* series of photographs,** 38, 108, *154, 155, 156–57*

Warhol, Andy, 55

Washburn, Alex, 34

Washburn, Annie, 91

Washington Grasslands, 208, *208–209, 210, 211, 212–13*

Watch World, 5, 17

Watts, Naomi, 113

Weinberg, Adam, 100

Weiss, Lois, 27

Weisz, Claire, 24, 34

West Chelsea, 4, 5–6; galleries, 4, 15, 26, 64, 87; rezoning, 52–53, 64–66, 82–83, 89, 90, 98, 273, *273*; *see also* Chelsea neighborhood

West Chelsea Arts Building, 26

West Side Cowboys, viii, 135, *135*

West Side Improvement Project, ix, 138, *138*, *139*

West Side Rail Line Development Foundation, x

West Side Rail Yards: background, 278; Giuliani's original plan for, 30; High Line access, 44, 50–51, 61, 108, 116; High Line considerations in planning process, 46–47, 52, 53, 67–68, 69–70, 86, 101–102, 104–105, 106; High Line section, 32–33, 278, *279*, *280*, *281*, *282–83*, *284*; HYDC plan without stadium, 101–102; Peter Obletz and his converted Pullman Car, *150*; proposed development plans, 112–13, 286, *286*, *287*, *288–89*; and stadium plan, 30, 46–47, 52, 53, 65, 67–68, 69–70, 86, *285*; *see also* Hudson Yards Development Commission (HYDC)

West Side Railroad Coalition, 20

West Village, 3

Whitney Museum, 100, *290*, 291

Wildflower Field, 260, *260–61*

Windows on the World, 11

Wingo, Doug, 34

Wintour, Anna, 113

Wood, Deb, 22

Woodner, Andrea, 24, 34

Woolco, 86–87

WORKac (architects), 276

World Trade Center, 10, 11, 34, 39–40

Yankee Stadium, 30

Zieman, John, 59

zoning, *see* rezoning

IMAGE CREDITS

3 Photographer unknown

9 Courtesy of Friends of the High Line

16 Courtesy of Friends of the High Line

28 Joel Sternfeld

36 Chris Payne

41 Courtesy of Friends of the High Line

48 Courtesy of Friends of the High Line

53 Courtesy of Friends of the High Line

64 Casey Jones, courtesy of Friends of the High Line

73 Courtesy of Friends of the High Line

81 Courtesy of Friends of the High Line

89 Joe Marianek

93 Courtesy of Friends of the High Line

101 Alex S. MacLean/Landslides Aerial Photography

109 David Kimelman

118 © Patrick McMullan

123 Iwan Baan

132–33 Stephen Wilkes

134 Photographer unknown

135 Courtesy of Kalmbach Publishing Company

136 Hugh Ferriss, originally published in *Architectural Forum*, 1927

137 Moses King, from *King's Views of New York*, 1908

138 Courtesy of Consolidated Rail Corporation

139 All images courtesy of Friends of the High Line

140 Photographer unknown

141 Courtesy of Kalmbach Publishing Company

142 Photographer unknown

143 James Shaughnessy

144 Photographer unknown

145 Courtesy of New York Rail Road Enthusiasts

146 Courtesy of Friends of the High Line

147 Abelardo Morell

148 Courtesy of Friends of the High Line

149, top   Jesse Chehak

149, bottom   Courtesy of Friends of the High Line

150 Peter Richards

151 Steven Holl

152 Courtesy of Friends of the High Line

153 Joel Sternfeld

154–55 All images by Joel Sternfeld

156–57 Joel Sternfeld

158–59 Courtesy of Friends of the High Line

160–61 Jonathan Flaum

162–63 All images courtesy of Friends of the High Line

164–65 Courtesy of Friends of the High Line

166–67 All images courtesy of Friends of the High Line

168–69 All images courtesy of Friends of the High Line

170–71 All images courtesy of Friends of the High Line

172–73 All images courtesy of Friends of the High Line

174–75 All images courtesy of Friends of the High Line

176–77 All images courtesy of Friends of the High Line

178 Terence Koh, courtesy of Friends of the High Line

179 All images by Tom Kletecka, courtesy of Friends of the High Line

180–81 All images by Tom Kletecka, courtesy of Friends of the High Line

182 Barry Munger

183, top   Barry Munger

183, bottom   © Patrick McMullan

184–85 All images © Patrick McMullan

186 Joan Garvin

187, top and bottom   All images © Patrick McMullan

188–89 Paula Scher

190–91 Spencer Tucker, Office of the Mayor

192–93 All images by Barry Munger

194 Barry Munger

195, top   Tim Schenck

195, bottom   Courtesy of Friends of the High Line

196, top   Courtesy of Friends of the High Line

196, bottom   Barry Munger

197 Tim Schenck

198 Barry Munger

199 Courtesy of Friends of the High Line

200–201 © Patrick McMullan

202–203 Barry Munger

204–205 All images by Barry Munger

206 Iwan Baan

207, top   James Corner Field Operations and Diller Scofidio + Renfro, courtesy of the City of New York

207, bottom   Iwan Baan

208–209, top   Barry Munger

208–209, bottom   Borja Martínez

210 Marcin Wichary

211 Iwan Baan

212–13, top   James Corner Field Operations and Diller Scofidio + Renfro, courtesy of the City of New York

212, bottom   Cristina Macaya

213, bottom   Amy Dreher

214–15 Iwan Baan

216–17 All images by Joan Garvin

218 Iwan Baan

219 Justin Lintz

220 Sean Walsh

221 Patrick Cullina

222–23 Tim Schenck

224, top   Claudia Berger, courtesy of Friends of the High Line

224, bottom   Brian D. Bumby

225 Nikole Bouchard

226–27 Iwan Baan

228–29 All images by Gary Sloman

230 All images by Iwan Baan

231, top   Barry Munger

231, bottom   Susan Micari

232–33 Iwan Baan

234 Juan Valentin

235, top   Mandee Johnson

235, bottom   John Korpics

236–37, top   Cristina Macaya

236, bottom   James Corner Field Operations and Diller Scofidio + Renfro, courtesy of the City of New York

237, bottom   Iwan Baan

238 Michael Pearce

239 Iwan Baan

240 Yuki Shingai

241 Juan Valentin

242 Cristina Macaya

243 Iwan Baan

244, top   Brian D. Bumby

244–45, bottom   Iwan Baan

245, top   Cristina Macaya

246 John Blough

247 Patrick Cullina

248 Barry Munger

249 Iwan Baan

250–51 All images by Barry Munger

252–53 All images by Iwan Baan

254–55 All images by Iwan Baan

256 Iwan Baan

257 Barry Munger

258–59 All images by Iwan Baan

260–61 Iwan Baan

262–63 All images by Iwan Baan

264 Iwan Baan

265, top   James Corner Field Operations and Diller Scofidio + Renfro, courtesy of the City of New York

265, bottom   Barry Munger

266–67 All images by Patrick Cullina

268 Patrick Cullina

269, top   Barry Munger

269, bottom   Claudia Berger, courtesy of Friends of the High Line

270–71 All images by Patrick Cullina

272 Courtesy of Friends of the High Line

273 All images courtesy of the New York City Department of City Planning

274 Nikolas Koening

275, upper left   Della Valle Bernheimer

275, upper right   © David Sundberg/Esto

275, lower left   Courtesy of High Line Development, LLC

275, lower right   Steve Oles–ADM Studio

276, upper left   Shigeru Ban Architects

276, upper right   Ateliers Jean Nouvel

276, lower left   Courtesy of Diane von Furstenberg

276, lower right   © Albert Vecerka/Esto

277 Hayes Davidson

278, upper left, middle, right   Barry Munger

278, bottom   Jesse Chehak

279 Alex S. MacLean/Landslides Aerial Photography

280, top   Alex S. MacLean/Landslides Aerial Photography

280, bottom   Barry Munger

281 Courtesy of Friends of the High Line

282–83 Joel Sternfeld

284 Courtesy of Google

285 Kohn Pederson Fox

286 Steven Holl Architects

287 Brookfield Office Properties

288–89 All images courtesy of The Related Companies

290 Renzo Piano Building Workshop in partnership with Cooper, Robertson & Partners

291 Renzo Piano Building Workshop and Beyer Blinder Belle, courtesy of Friends of the High Line

292–93 Iwan Baan

294–95 All images by Josiah Lau

296 Karen Blumberg

297 Joan Garvin

298 Joan Garvin

299, top   Karen Blumberg

299, bottom   Courtesy of Friends of the High Line

300 Kim Beck

301, top and bottom   Jason Mandella

302–303, top   Jason Mandella

302–303, bottom   Luke Stettner

304 David Kimelman

305, top   Courtesy of Friends of the High Line

305, bottom   David Kimelman

306–307, top   Patrick Cullina

FRIENDS OF THE HIGH LINE

Friends of the High Line is the nonprofit conservancy responsible for maintaining the High Line, under a license agreement with the New York City Department of Parks & Recreation. Friends of the High Line provides more than 90 percent of the High Line's annual operating budget and is responsible for maintenance of the park.

There are many ways that you can be a part of this project. To learn more, please visit **www.thehighline.org**.

PUBLIC PROGRAMS
Friends of the High Line offers free and low-cost public programs, including talks, films, performances, tours, and family activities.

PUBLIC ART
High Line Art commissions temporary, large-scale, and site-specific works of public art for the park, offering a platform for visual, performance, or sound-based art by both emerging and established artists.

MEMBERSHIP
The High Line depends on the support of its members to keep the park thriving in every season. When you join Friends of the High Line, you provide crucial support for the maintenance and operation of the park, allowing us to hire gardeners and maintenance crews to ensure that the High Line is in peak condition. Members receive a High Line newsletter, discounts at local stores, and other special benefits. For more information, please contact members@thehighline.org.

FOR MORE INFORMATION
For park hours, stair and elevator locations, directions, and local transportation, visit www.thehighline.org.

Follow us on Facebook, on Twitter, and through our e-newsletter.